Walking with Dog

What Man's Best Friend Can Teach Us about God

TOM VINT

iUniverse, Inc.
Bloomington

Walking with Dog
What Man's Best Friend Can Teach Us about God

iUniverse books may be ordered through booksellers or by contacting:

iUniverse
1663 Liberty Drive
Bloomington, IN 47403
www.iuniverse.com
1-800-Authors (1-800-288-4677)

ISBN: 978-1-4502-9077-7 (sc)
ISBN: 978-1-4502-9075-3 (ebook)
ISBN: 978-1-4502-9076-0 (dj)

Library of Congress Control Number: 2011904703

Printed in the United States of America

iUniverse rev. date: 5/27/2011

Contents

Tom and Lexi in a good place

Preface

A few years ago, I was sitting on my porch with a glass of iced tea, a good book in hand, and my faithful Labrador curled up at my feet. I realized that was one of those special moments we have, where a feeling of contentment comes over you. Life is good. What made the moment so special? It wasn't so much the tea, which I consume in abundance with much delight. It wasn't the book, although I enjoy reading time whenever it comes. It had much more to do with the dog, and the bond we had developed.

Thankfully, I have learned the pleasure of enjoying and appreciating my moments of contentment. One thing that remained a constant with these moments was my faithful companion. It took me years to realize the simple thing I will share with you in this book. The simple thing was right in front of me the whole time, yet I missed it by running past it over and over in the race of life in which too many of us get caught up. Sitting there with my best friend—who respected me in all I did, and even loved me for all of my flaws—I became aware of how I had been doing things so wrong. I had to see the love my faithful companion showed me—no matter my mood or disregard of her—to realize what I was supposed to do and how I was supposed to do it. Trust me when I say that being respected and loved unconditionally is a great feeling. Seeing unconditional love, as shown to us by our four-legged friends, should teach all of us a lesson in how we are supposed to treat each other. Could you imagine how great life would be if we could respect and love one another with as much completeness as dogs do for their owners? They protect us as if saying "Nobody will hurt you on my watch." They serve us with undeniable obedience. They forgive us without hesitation or rebuke—even when we occasionally mistreat or scold them. They show us incredible respect by seeking our approval in every action. All they ask in return is to be loved. A simple rub on the head or "good dog" is all they live for. To love and be loved is their purpose. Imagine if we all could be as obedient, forgiving, serving, and affectionate to one another. How perfect would that world be?

I was given my first Labrador retriever in the mid-1970s and, with the exception of only a few months between dogs, we have had a Lab in our home ever since. I have shared a lot of great stories with fellow dog owners over the years about how these wonderful creatures bring so much to our lives. Dogs have become cherished members of many families.

Whether they are lapdogs or any of the giant breeds, dogs are known as man's best friend for a reason. Simply put, they just are. I have learned so much from my dogs, including how to be a better parent, spouse, and friend. They taught me something else that surprised me: my relationships with my dogs mirrored my spiritual relationship with God in so many ways. I was once a puppy, having to learn the ways of my Master. I didn't always do everything correctly, and I was disciplined. I found joy in learning to obey, and reward for doing life right. Most of all, I learned about love.

Those of us who have been blessed with truly special relationships in our lives have spoken of love for us and our love for others. Everybody wants to be loved—at least on some level. It is human nature—a part of us that longs to belong. We are made for relationships.

It was the only time in the Bible's creation story in Genesis that God said something wasn't good. Adam was alone. God created Eve, man's helpmate. Human bonding was formed. Then everything was very good. Relationships are very good.

Relationships also are behind the psychology for having pets. I think of it as a supplement to human-to-human relationships, and sometimes more than merely a supplement. Having a pet is a form of community, right? Having a dog, or even a cat, is a bonding relationship with an animal. For dogs, it is a pack mentality. They love community. Cats? Well, the jury is still out on them, as some may be demonically possessed as I suspect my daughter's cat may be. On the other hand, they do provide comfort for a number of people.

There is no question that we find value in our good relationships. We all love to be loved, even if just by a little creature with hairy skin.

The English language has a number of meanings for the word "love." We certainly can love our spouses, our parents, and our children. We love our friends, neighbors, maybe even our in-laws. We love pizza, movies, a walk on the beach, a rainy day nap. We love it when good things happen to us. Obviously, those references to love have slightly different meanings. There are degrees of fondness involved.

In the English language, love can be a noun or a verb. It is no wonder why some people trying to learn English are so confused about a number of our words. Love is just one of those complex, multiple-meaning, yet often-used words used in so many contexts.

The ancient Greek language perhaps can help us out a little more in understanding those layers of love. Greek scholars have noted the language has at least three words that represent types or levels of maturing love. The first is "eros," which is the sexual or romantic type of love, from which our modern word "erotic" is derived. That is a physical attraction drawing one person to another. This type of love is more self-gratifying, however. The visual or physical experience brings us pleasure. We love that. It can often be descriptive of the early stages of a bond between two people. While eros love may be a strong influence for a young couple, for instance, it seldom is the level of love that sustains a long-term relationship.

Two other Greek words are often used in the Bible, particularly in the New Testament as Jesus teaches His disciples about new levels of human bonding and commitment.

The Greek word "phileo" is a more brotherly type of love, as in Philadelphia, the City of Brotherly Love. This is the friendship type of love we have for our circle of acquaintances, the people we like. We call them friends. This is a higher level of love, involving less self and more mutual sharing. It can be a very strong bond. It is the type of love that brings happiness when your friends or family are happy. You find satisfaction and appreciation in more things outside of yourself.

The third type of love is the deepest, self-sacrificing variety. The Greek word "agape" is used for this type, which is reflected in the truly strong love a parent has for a child, or the love for a mate. While it can include the emotions of "eros" and "phileo" love, it goes much deeper. True "agape" love is something really special to share. It is a love not resulting from any necessary or special conditions of reciprocation. I once heard this type of love described as always wanting the very best for someone else—even at one's own expense.

Agape love is willingness to sacrifice, even die, for another. It is an all-out, hold-nothing-back type of love. We all have heard stories of soldiers sacrificing their lives to save their fellow soldiers. We have heard of mothers or fathers willing to put their lives on the line for their children.

Most of us who have a Christian relationship with our heavenly Father believe God has an unconditional love for us. The Bible tells us that through John 3:16: "God so loved the world that He gave His only begotten Son, that whoever believes in Him shall not perish but have everlasting life." Jesus went to the cross to pay for our sins because of His agape love for mankind, God's greatest creation.

I believe that type of unconditional love is really the best type to receive and share, but it is sometimes hard to grasp or define for those of us who live "normal" lives. What is it to be loved unconditionally? How do we put a face on that? How do you explain it to someone? There are a lot of people in the world who can hear the words but can't grasp the concept without some visual picture, something real and tangible. They need an example.

Perhaps God provided just such an example we everyday people can view up close. It could be just as close as our walk with our dogs. Yes, our family dogs.

There are many instances in the Bible where God used the unexpected to make a point and accomplish His purposes. One of the giants of the faith was Moses. He killed a man and stuttered, yet he led God's people out of Egyptian captivity. Jesus was born to a poverty-stricken couple instead of into a royal court, yet He changed the world. Nobody saw that coming in His day.

I believe God has a great sense of humor to use the unexpected. I see that in my own life. My shy nature drives me to find a seat in a room closest to the back where no one will notice me. Instead, God led me to stand in front of an adult Sunday school class as a teacher. I took a 7:30 a.m. mandatory speech class in college because I knew no self-respecting college kid would get up that early. There were five of us in that class who had the same idea, but I still needed a lectern to help steady shaking hands and knees.

I think God chuckles at what He first did to me in the late 1990s when I was asked to teach a class of adults, several of whom had studied the Bible for years. That was intimidating. Still, God peeled me off the wall to help Him make a difference in someone's life. It is not so much what He did to me as what He has done through me. I have been called to help train His people. If He can call a shy writer to do that, why not use good family dogs to show us the kind of love He wants us to share with each other?

I have considered many potential parallels in how we interact with God and how our dogs interact with their masters. They all start with love.

Just sit and watch some time when a dog is around his or her master. See the mannerisms and the looks the animal gives the master. There are looks of respect, reverence, appreciation, longing to belong, dedication, and even of agape love. They want to be close, in contact, be reassured of the relationship.

In my household, we have grown up with a number of good dogs to bless our lives. I have had four wonderful Labradors over the past four-plus decades—Boo Boo, Pepper, Sadie, and Lexi. They all brought something special to our family. We loved our dogs, but I didn't fully realize just how much love and meaning each of those furry friends gave us until they left us. The first three have died. Lexi is our current companion and constant reminder of genuine bonding.

I don't know of many people who have had dogs for a number of years who could say after the time of their passing that those animals didn't leave an empty place in their homes and hearts. Good dogs become like members of the family. I have often told people that I wished my kids would mind me as well as my dogs do. I was only half-kidding. My wife and I had two really great kids. The dogs were awfully special, too. Our kids will tell anybody that the dogs really did obey better.

When we lost Sadie, the third of those loving companions, we received a number of sympathy letters, e-mails, and comments from our family and friends. They were dog people and knew the unique bond a family can have with a four-legged member of your pack. They knew how much we loved that old dog and the special part she played in our family. Those people made us ponder the wonder, delight, forgiveness, and love displayed to us by these phenomenal creations of our God in heaven.

Most of our four-legged family members display an unconditional love that could serve us well as an example of the love we should have for each other. It is the love that goes beyond friendship to sacrifice. It is the love Jesus showed in His painful trek to the cross.

One of the e-mails after Sadie's death came from a friend, Brian Haston. It read:

Dear Tom,

I'm sorry to hear about your loss, Tom. Last November, we had to put our Lab of fourteen years down. The vet said it was his heart. "Beau" (BoBo) was a faithful companion, floor pillow for my children, watchdog, and someone who always made us feel special. I remember being in your Sunday school class a few years back and bringing up the subject of our pets. I don't remember the exact words, but I remember saying that I thank God for our dogs and believe that some of the best in human qualities are demonstrated by our pets. They love us even when we have not been so loving to them. They don't hold a grudge and forgive us immediately when we've wronged them. They want nothing more than to be with us and the highlight of their day was just to have us come home. It may be a stretch, but I can see in our pets an example of the love our Father in Heaven gives to us. I'm thankful for the animals God created, especially those so well suited to share our lives with.

With kind regards,
Brian Haston

Mandy, our daughter with her own Labrador, Bella, captured the thought perfectly. "It all kind of reminds me of the time when I told you about God and Adam. How (Pastor) Billy (Coburn) explained to us that God was looking for Adam in the Garden even after he ate the (forbidden) fruit. Even though God knew Adam had eaten the fruit, He still wanted to go on His usual scheduled walk. But Adam was hiding (like we can hide from God). The point being that God just wants to be close to us and walk with us and talk with us, right?" How right she was.

"Well, then I took my little Bella for a walk that same day. I had a thought and sat and talked with her like she was God. 'Walking with Dog,' I call it," she said. "She wags her tail, hangs out her tongue, listens intently, and tilts her head from side to side, hanging on my every word. She doesn't often say anything back—and even if she does, I don't always understand its meaning. But she listens and cares and wants to be there with me—no matter what I've done to her or to anyone else that day. Walking with dog; walking with God. Is that why they have all of the same letters in their names? Dog … God? I do believe there is a connection there," Mandy said.

"They are examples of God's love in the flesh and how blessed we are to have such an example in our lives, even if it is temporary. It's no wonder we feel such pain when they leave us to be with God in heaven. Imagine how painful it would be *knowing* God and then having Him stripped from our lives. Now *that* would be some pain and loneliness, wouldn't it? Knowing God, and then losing God. I think that is why it hurts so much to lose our puppies. Just like everyone is saying—they are *awesome* examples of God's love."

Mandy added, "God knows what He is doing. I'm so glad we know the Lord. He has blessed us with His presence in the Spirit, and gives us 'dog people' a reminder of His love in the flesh through our dogs."

God gave us our four-legged furry friends for a reason. I hope you can experience both loves: a loyal companion here and the one of our graceful Host in heaven. My prayers are for this book to enlighten you to our intended purpose, and show how our faithful companions give us a living example of how to accomplish it. It begins and ends with love. May this book help you understand love, feel love, and show love as never before. Love is what leads to a perfect day. Giving and receiving love starts with you. It starts in your heart. My hope is that you will see—through the examples given to my family by our four-legged blessings—how loving and receiving God's love can improve your life so you too can have your own perfect world.

Puppy ready to start

In The Beginning

Where does a great story begin? We all have stories to tell. I have become a believer that God puts us in different places in this world to live a story, figure out how He became involved in it all, and finally to share all that with others. It is called our living witness. It is our life. We all have such a story—some of us just take a lot longer to figure it out. Some of us take longer still to get to the point where we can begin to share it with others.

During the 1970s, I was an outdoor writer for the Lincoln, Nebraska, newspapers. Not long out of college and just finished with a two-year stint in the military, my young wife and I settled into our new life just a few hours from our native home in central Iowa.

As an outdoor writer, I had opportunities to interview and spend time with a number of people in the outdoor-recreation world. Outdoor writers write about the great outdoors—hunting, fishing, camping, and the like. It is a pretty nice job most of the time. My job basically allowed me to do things most people have to take vacations to enjoy. I was paid for it. Despite the facts that I was always looking for a story and generally carrying around bulky cameras for illustrations, it was a lot of fun to write about people enjoying the out-of-doors. I made a lot of friends over those years.

Of particular fascination to me were the field-trial-dog trainers and what they could do with their dogs. It amazed me how those retrieving dogs could be directed by a whistle and hand signals from what seemed to be hundreds of yards away. It was delightful to watch the dogs work the air with their gifted noses to help guide them to a targeted bird. It impressed me greatly how the dogs did all this with joy in bringing the prize back to their masters. The dogs' tails were up and wagging with their delight in doing just what they were born to do. I enjoyed writing those stories about men and women and their dogs. I dreamed of the day when I could have a dog of my own, a dog like those.

When my wife and I moved to Lincoln, we lived in a small two-bedroom duplex owned by a wonderful couple who took pity on us. They could relate to our just coming out of the military with no money in our pockets. They had done the same thing themselves a few years earlier. They also apparently thought we'd be good neighbors, which was important since they lived in the other side of their tandem home. They were delightful people with two young daughters. One of their rules was no pets, but that didn't bother us because we didn't have one—at least not yet.

Several months into the new job, I went to lunch with a friend and a couple of sales representatives for a number of outdoor sporting goods products. During our conversations on a number of subjects, one of those gentlemen, Don Bader, mentioned something about field trialing his Labrador retrievers. He had been raising Labs and apparently had some very good ones. Several had earned field-champion status for winning field trials. It was a measuring stick for top-quality dogs. Good bloodlines are very valuable.

It caught my interest and drew us into a lengthy conversation on the rewards of well-bred dogs, training techniques, abilities of the dogs to do so many things, and just about everything else related to dogs. In my writings, I had witnessed the attributes of many gundog breeds. I compared all the things I desired in a dog—versatility in the ability to hunt many types of birds and in various conditions. I also wanted a dog that would be great for the family my wife and I had not yet started. I came to the conclusion that a Labrador retriever would best fit all the things I wanted in a good dog when I was ready to get one.

It is a marvelous breed—smart, eager to please, trainable, versatile, and a wonderful family and service dog. Labs seem to have it all. I had read up on many breeds I thought would fit the versatility I desired. I found many breeds that have great characteristics, and I certainly don't want to diminish the joy any of them can bring an owner, but a Lab, I decided, was the one I wanted.

During my conversation with Don, I mentioned something about how I would love to try training such a dog someday. I had heard how much easier it was to train a dog when it came from good bloodlines. My new friend confirmed that paying for better breeding provides dividends in easier training. He noted that field-trial dogs, much like seeing-eye dogs, are bred for desired traits such as temperament, scenting ability, trainability, speed, size, and so on. Yes, the Labrador is a great breed. Okay, now I *really* wanted one.

Don said one of his dogs was about to have a litter of pups and asked if I would like one.

I was momentarily speechless. The thought of owning such an animal was a great temptation. When I regained my composure, however, I tried to explain that it would be wonderful, but it was not in our family budget to feed a pet, let alone buy a purebred dog with such good breeding.

Don said that wasn't a problem, but I continued to graciously decline. My wife and I were still trying to put enough money together to buy furniture for our home. In truth, it was embarrassing to tell Don just how poor we were. We really had come out of the military without any money. As much as I would have loved a dog, it wasn't the time. We couldn't afford one.

We left the restaurant and, other than an occasional daydream of such a dog, I didn't think much more about the conversation. A few months later, however, there came a call from the Lincoln Airport baggage department. I had a package to pick up, and it needed to be picked up soon. I had no idea what the clerk was talking about. We had not ordered anything from anybody. He said there was a little dog kennel there, and it had my name on it. It wasn't empty. We needed to pick up our package. When I asked where it came from, the clerk said, "St. Louis, from a Don Bader."

I called my wife and said we needed to run out to the airport. We had only one car, and she had it at her new job as a bank teller. We didn't know what to expect when we arrived to get the package, other than the obvious—the little dog kennel likely housed a little dog.

My wife was not a dog person. Her family had cats. She wasn't ready for a pet, and we had no clue about where it was going to stay. Remember the no-pet stipulation at the duplex?

When we arrived at the baggage claim, we were directed to the small kennel in the back. We bent down and opened the door of our package. There she was—a black shadow plastered against the back of this frightening cage, shaking in fear, and uncertain about what had just happened to her world. Don had sent us one of his Labradors.

My wife pulled the trembling pup out of the kennel and wrapped her in her arms. She cuddled the new baby all the way home. A bond was formed instantly. How can you not fall in love with a little Lab puppy with those big "cow" eyes and a desire to shower you with kisses for rescuing her from the great unknown?

We really didn't know what to do. I had to call Don to say that I'd have to send her back. Besides, we couldn't afford to buy a dog like this. He said something to the effect that he "wouldn't take her back. You can't afford the shipping costs, for one thing. Besides, she was a gift, and the pedigree papers are in the mail. She has championship field-trial bloodlines. This is a valuable little puppy. Enjoy your first real dog."

That was our beginning with Boo Boo. The name was significant from the standpoint that her arrival was a "boo boo" for us, at least right then. And we still had the no-pet rule to face when we arrived home.

After a little explanation that this was not really our doing, our landlords let us bring the puppy home with the understanding that we'd find someplace else for her quickly. Boo was a happy puppy, and she was doing fine in her new surroundings until the landlord, his wife, and their two young children came home from a little outing a few days later. I was playing with the pup in the yard when the neighbors and their two little girls arrived. Boo saw the little three-year-old girl, who let out a happy shriek at seeing the puppy. Boo raced to greet her … but didn't stop.

This ten-week-old puppy leaped into what she perceived as "waiting" arms, and steamrolled the poor little girl. The happy shriek turned into one of terror. It was more crying out in surprise than injury, but the deed was done. Boo deflated at the little girl's feet. The puppy recognized she had done something terribly wrong. She never jumped on a child after that day, but the pup now had to go somewhere else immediately. That was the landlord's order.

Some coworker friends at the newspaper agreed to take Boo for a little while until we figured something out. They had a nice house, a big garage, a large backyard, and all the things a puppy could use. None of us realized, however, how a free-running, ten-week-old Labrador puppy could rearrange a garage when left unattended. In a matter of days, we were looking at replacing a piece of drywall she had tried to dig through and the insulating strip that formerly graced the bottom of the garage door.

Boo didn't like to be left alone, and she was digging her way out to find her people. We had not yet learned that putting a puppy in a kennel when left unattended for a few hours is much safer for the puppy and for its environment. It also could save a lot of time when you don't have to take inventory of things potentially digested that could be dangerous for a pup. Like new parents with a first baby, we had a lot to learn about raising our first real dog.

Boo led us to quickly act on buying a house near our duplex. We had watched a small house come on the market and had some interest in it prior to the arrival of the pup. The house sold quickly and we were disappointed we had missed out. Within days, however, it came back on the market. The first deal apparently fell through. We put in an offer, and miraculously found financing to carry the entire cost of the $17,000 purchase. It wasn't a really expensive house, even by standards of that day, but it met our needs at the time. We could move in by month's end. Our first dog led us to buy our first house, a small two-bedroom home with a large fenced backyard. It was some beginning.

As we look back now more than three decades later, we realize how much a hand God must have had in all that. He brought us this special little dog—which didn't stay little long, and led us to buy our first home with really wonderful neighbors. And they liked our puppy, too. How could you not? Boo Boo was a delight for all of us. She was a heart-warmer, such a loving puppy that the neighbors had to like us so they could spend more time with her. I'd like to think we were good people, but we had this puppy with big brown eyes and a ready wag to her tail any time somebody came around. She invited anyone to pet her. It was as if God had provided a happy little icebreaker that opened doors of friendship for those near us.

Pepper and Tigger share beanbag

Just Walking with You

For those of us who have been in love with someone, there is a period of time, often early in the relationship, when you can't get enough of the other person. You want to be around them all the time. You can talk to them for hours. You find pleasure just to look at them or hear the sound of their voice.

So it is with a good dog. However, unlike most of our human relationships, the Labs I have had never seemed to lose that feeling of wanting to be with us. I find that amazing sometimes when I know I am not in the best of moods and won't be the best of company. Those four-legged creatures still want to be around us. My wife and kids might not want to share my time and space, but the dogs do. I wish more of us could be wired like that.

There was a great cartoon I clipped out once to remind me of those days when I, like the little girl in the comic, wanted to post a sign that said, "Leave me alone. Don't talk to me. I'm in a rotten mood." The girl's dog came up to the chair where she was sulking, and when she looked up to see him, the dog lathered her with several big, wet kisses. The last frame of the cartoon had the dog curled up in the little girl's lap. Her rotten mood had disappeared. There is something about big, wet kisses that tend to soften even a hardened heart.

Boo had such a great personality. She was so eager to learn and be with us that it was hard to go anywhere without her. I began reading as many dog-training books as I could find. One of the best I ever picked up was *Hey, Pup, Fetch It Up* by Bill Tarrant. One of the things he mentioned about training the best dogs was spending a lot of time with them. That wasn't too tough to do with Boo Boo.

We had a big, old Chevy Impala, and her favorite place to ride was in the back window. It wasn't a big deal when she was a pup, but, as I mentioned, she didn't stay small for long.

Boo was what I learned later to be a larger strain of Labrador believed to have been bred in Newfoundland. Those Labs tend to be taller, generally thinner, and more energetic than the shorter, more docile strain of Labs bred for fishing boat use and later refined for hunting and retrieving by English breeders.

Boo grew quickly and soon nearly filled the back window of that rather substantial car. She drew a lot of double takes from fellow motorists; most initially thought she was just a really big bobbing-head stuffed animal that was popular in those days. People would pass, honk, and wave to us. They would offer a big smile while shaking their heads and pointing to the back window.

Boo also learned quickly to work the system. She was just as smart as she was friendly. Georgie had never owned a dog during the time I knew her, at least not a housedog. She was in agreement with my dad, who said dogs were supposed to be outside animals, but then he raised us and our childhood dogs on an acreage. There was a lot of room to be outside.

What I wanted as my training goal, however, was to prove to people that a great hunting dog also could be a great indoor dog and family pet. I always felt dogs were meant to be companions. It pained me to think of wasting all of their love in an outside kennel. Dogs, in my opinion, are meant to be *with* us.

At my wife's demand, Boo first was limited to the basement of our little home. The basement steps came up to the kitchen, and Boo would lie on the top step with her head on the tile floor. Her sad eyes would follow my wife's every move while she worked in the kitchen. The pup would occasionally offer a deep sigh or a quiet whimper to softly share her displeasure at being kept so far away from her "parents." Apparently, six feet was a lot of separation. We didn't have a very large kitchen.

"Okay, it's all right for her to be in the kitchen, but not on the carpet." Cute puppies can melt hearts.

Boo wasn't quite satisfied with just the kitchen, either. After all, we didn't spend all of our time there. She would sleep at the edge of the kitchen tile floor and somehow could "magically" stretch in mid-nap. Remarkably, she would end up on the carpet. We'd catch her and push her back to the tile. No matter how much correction or nudging back off the carpet, she would always go back to fake her nap, stretch, and there she was. Even having her very own rug didn't matter; there was even more deep sighing and whimpering.

"Okay, she can come in on the carpet." Boo was one happy young dog, curled up at our feet with no more problems in the world. The sighs and whimpers were exchanged for a regular happy tail thump on the carpeted floor next to where one of us was sitting.

The reality was that she wanted to be with us and keep us in her sight. It should be no surprise that such a gregarious pack animal wants to have company. She, and every other dog we've had, had the same need, the same want. They wanted to be close to the ones they love.

God created us for relationships, and good dogs are reminders of that very point. They are pack animals and relish life in a crowd. They love family—if they can touch you, it's even better.

Boo was okay if she was just touching your chair or your leg if you were on the couch. If we were dining, she was under my chair, until the kids came along. She then found their place at the table had more benefits from little people learning how to handle food. If we were sleeping, she was in bed with us, sleeping on my legs or between my wife and me. She was such a good dog it was easy to spoil her.

I didn't roll over in my sleep very often in those days with the growing dog on my legs. That ended, however, when Boo reached about eighty pounds as a two-year-old and stretched one night while sleeping on the bed with her back to me. My very pregnant wife was pushed right out of bed. Boo was no longer welcome to sleep between us.

The big dog had to settle for a rug beside the bed. She didn't like that much. She moped for a few nights with a handful of sighs and whimpers until she figured things had changed permanently. Still, she moved her rug as close as she could to our bed, getting as close as she could, still touching.

The loving nature of dogs to want to touch—cuddle, nudge, lick (kiss)—is an example for us as well. We are so much better as loving members of our families when we touch in love. Marriage counselors and therapists have said couples have fewer problems if they spend more time cuddling, nudging, and kissing. That certainly makes sense.

I firmly believe God made us to be touchy-feely creatures. Our hands and lips are sensory beacons that can help us assure each other that we're okay. "I'm here," or "I love you."

Jesus was big on touching. He would touch to heal the blind, the lame, the sick, the untouchable lepers. His power was great enough, however, that He didn't need to touch. Several people were healed just by His word. Still, Jesus touched.

Society of His day frowned on such touching. It made Him ceremonially "unclean." It was a special problem for the religious elite, who didn't understand Jesus. Still, He touched and did good deeds as only He could. People touched Him and felt the miraculous surge of power that only God could conduct. There is healing in His touch, and His touch is really, really good. This God-man among us shared His love often through touch.

All of our dogs reinforced that desire to be physically touched, but perhaps none did better than our fourth Lab, Lexi. She is a great toucher. She continually seeks a physical touch. She is one of Bella's babies and had a special bond with her sister, Gabbie. Those two were seldom out of each other's quick-touch range. They would sleep together in the litter box from birth and go to each other's rescue when littermates would pick on one or the other. They would even chew on opposite ends of the same stick or bone.

The two pups spent several weeks at our house, separated from the rest of the litter. They never took a nap without touching each other. One day when Gabbie needed to go outside, I opened the door to the backyard, and she bounced out. Lexi apparently didn't need to go so she sat down next to me. Gabbie didn't want to be alone outside so she stepped back into the house, grabbed Lexi by her collar, and pulled her out. That was when I realized how smart these little puppies were and just how strong was the bond between them. They were eleven weeks old.

God desires that kind of strong bond with us. He doesn't want us to go anywhere without Him, and once we recognize the value in that relationship, we certainly don't want to go anywhere without Him. Like Lexi and Gabbie, we should be joined at the hip with our heavenly Father. It is a bond of security, comfort, safety, and love. It is a new, special-relationship, "I want to be with you a lot more" type of love. Sometimes we have to venture out into the dark, scary yard, but we know from His Word that God never lets us go alone. He's holding our hands, touching us always.

When Gabbie went to her permanent home in California with our son, Lexi would come tell us she needed a touch, which was, and still is, often. She sits in front of us, puts her head on our chair or lap and looks at us with her soft, dark eyes. If we try to ignore her, she squirms closer to our legs so we have to notice. When we reach out to scratch her head or nose, she closes her eyes with a contented squint as if she is experiencing the greatest pleasure she could ever experience—a surge of miraculous power from the master to heal her tender spirit. Often she will sigh in a contented manner. There is a need being met. Life is good. The master loves me.

It is a great lesson from dogs on the joy of touch, the need for touch, and the power of touch. It has been found that newborn babies do much better when they are cuddled. One Chinese study found that babies who are not touched or held tend to struggle in their developing new life. There is peace and comfort in cuddling. All is good. Somebody loves me.

Don't let adults fool you. They need loving touch, too. There are more than a few health experts who say our American society has lost a little something in its views of touching. We've become something of an arm's-length society.

Dogs crave touch and remind you of their need if they are being denied. We have never had a dog outgrow the need to be touched in love. I've never been around many adults who didn't enjoy a loving touch, either.

At our church in Omaha, we would hold hands at the end of the service to pray as a congregation. An elderly woman once said it was her favorite time of the week. She lived alone, and it was the only time anyone lovingly touched her. She received a lot of hugs after that when people found out about her need.

Medical studies have found people are healthier and heal more quickly when they receive loving touch. Do you think God knew something about that when He created us as touchy-feely beings?

A number of colleges around the nation have ongoing studies to try to decipher the health benefits of animal-human relationships. Some have found the association lowers blood pressure and can cause the body to produce feel-good hormones for both the dog and the human companion.

There are groups of professionals and volunteers who take dogs to nursing homes and rehabilitation centers because of the undeniable emotional—and sometimes physical—benefits to patients. There is something about having a calm, loving dog putting his or her head in your lap that makes the world right, at least for a short time.

There is a wrong kind of touch, too. The touch of abuse is not welcomed. It breaks a trust. God did not intend this for any of us—or for our pets.

Pepper, our second Lab, came to us a little later in her life. Several months after we lost Boo to cancer, we decided it was time to find another Lab to give life to our household. Pepper was nearly nine months old when I purchased her from a friend of a friend, who reportedly had a good line of Labradors. We didn't know her history up until that period in her life, but she apparently had been mistreated by someone.

Pepper would shy away from men, especially anyone with facial hair. She would dash to another room if anyone picked up a flyswatter. She was very protective of her food dish and would snarl or snap if anyone tried to take it from her or even refill it while she was eating. That is a sign of insecurity. Pepper didn't trust. She didn't want any part of touch in her first few weeks with us.

We had to build trust with Pepper. We had to show her we were safe. If I had to discipline her—as in breaking the snarling, snapping habit around food, particularly with young kids in the house—I would follow it up with a love session of hugs and petting.

The discipline was to never swat her with anything. She was way too fragile for that. I would grab her to keep her from possibly biting and roll her on her back. I had to be firm, but not abusive. I held her on her back until she yielded, understanding that I was the boss, and I wasn't going to tolerate bad behavior on her part. When she relaxed, she was given reassurance that she was still okay with us. She was going to be loved—just not uncontrolled.

Once we were able to break through to her, and once she knew we cared for her, she also was a great lover.

With Pepper, we had help from an unexpected source—a cat. I had to learn from Pepper to enjoy that particular creation of God. I've never been a cat person. Tigger, a cute little gray-striped kitten, was not an easy cat with which to build a bond. He had an attitude. In his youth, he didn't like people and didn't want anybody to mess with him. He really didn't like dogs much, either.

We had picked up the tiny, cute little critter as a present for my wife's mother, Wanda, who loved cats and had a little Sheltie. Wanda expected her little dog to find good company in this little cat. However, Tigger, in spite of his small stature, so harassed the meek-mannered Sheltie that the dog hid behind the sofa. The dog, which was several times larger than this kitten, didn't come out from hiding for two days. My mother-in-law said she couldn't keep the kitty.

We brought Tigger back to our home, where my wife had kept him for a few days before giving him to her mother. Our children had been very allergic to their friends' cats, but shorthaired Tigger didn't seem to bother them at all. My wife said the kitty could have a home with us. The look on her face convinced me that the executive decision had been made. Besides, she figured there wasn't much this bite-sized kitten could do to a nearly year-old Labrador that towered over him. He could pick on that Lab all day long and it wouldn't matter a whole lot.

Pepper loved Tigger for his attitude because it was nonthreatening to her. In a way, Tigger brought Pepper out of her shell. This poor, frightened puppy tried to ignore all of us. Pepper and Tigger could relate to each other in that regard.

Tigger, who was so very small and looked so cuddly, acted as if he hated to have anybody pay attention to him. He would try to avoid my wife, the cat person, who would pick him up and hug him. Interestingly, he hated even more being totally ignored, which is what Pepper and I did to him.

To make certain he wasn't ignored totally by the dog and me, Tigger would attack the big black puppy, holding onto her leg as she would try to walk away. It soon became a game, and they never tired of playing it for all of Pepper's nine years with us. If Tigger pretended to be too tired to play, Pepper would grab the cat by one of his legs and drag him across the carpet until he was ready to scrap back.

They fed off each other, gaining confidence in themselves and in others. It was good to have a friend, and people were okay, too. Pepper would even share her beanbag bed and water dish with that ornery little cat. They were family.

Later in Pepper's life, when illness caused her to struggle with comfort, Tigger still would go up and nudge his friend. We called it Tigger's head-butt, like what football players do to each other with helmets on. Tigger started greeting us at the top of the stairs when we came home. The dog was on the top step, anxiously waiting for us to climb to her. The equally excited cat was poking through the banister railing with a welcoming meow. Tigger's head-butt was his welcome. He was touching. The dog waited for her turn for a welcomed petting when we topped the steps.

After Pepper's passing, the little cat with an attitude would actually crawl into our laps for a touch. Tigger found out that he needed a touch. This little cat started acting like our dogs. He missed his friend just as we did. He needed comfort for his loss, too.

Tigger was around all twelve years we had our next Labrador, Sadie. The cat-dog relationship continued with this new friend, but after Sadie died, Tigger's health deteriorated also. He left us a few weeks later.

Touch is an amazing thing. A safe touch can bring cats with an attitude or abused puppies out of their shells—and it can do the same for people.

Our dogs can sense when some people are uncomfortable with them. Sadie was great at that. She came along several months after Pepper and would rival Boo as probably the most gentle of our Labs.

Sadie and Boo made friends easily. They would warmly greet anyone who came to the house—as long as we were home. Both generally made the rounds of the guests and waited until the welcome petting was accomplished before moving on to the next person.

If someone shied away from Sadie, she would remember and return to their feet as if to say, "It's okay. I'll bond with you anyway. I'm safe. You can trust me. You must be somebody who needs a touch."

Mandy said it well, "I like to think God is working through our dogs. It seems Bella knows when I am stressed or sad and comes to me and offers her 'hug.' Just as God offers us His peace and comfort, it is those times I find comfort in my furry friend—comfort in her quiet moments of snuggles and hugs."

My dogs taught me the blessing of a hug. Lexi tries to put her paws on you and climb in your lap. She can't get close enough. She did that from the day she could first get on all four legs and bounce a little.

She would head to anybody sitting down and try to crawl into his or her lap. She found comfort there. It works for a ten-week-old puppy, but not so much for a full-grown Lab. She struggles with good manners regarding keeping her paws on the floor.

There are some visitors to our home who are not dog people. They don't relish a big dog trying to climb into their lap. They don't understand she is trying to say hi in her loving manner.

So we had to work on tempering that paw action and a little too much nuzzling from our newest girl because she didn't know how big she was getting. She still wants to be a lapdog and enjoys those moments when we get down on the floor with her so she can hug us. She wants to get closer. She loves to hug.

Lexi apparently has the sensitivity that Sadie had concerning people who are leery of dogs. We had a group of people from our adult Sunday school class over for dinner one evening. A new member of the class and her friend showed up and received one of Lexi's "there's somebody I don't know here" greeting. She lets out a "big dog" bark, then runs to the front door and jumps vertically—almost eyeball to eyeball to even the tallest of guests. The little girl can jump.

My wife scurried to let the two ladies in the door. Lexi, of course, tried to wag a greeting nearby. Then the new class member said she was not a dog person and dogs really bothered her. We pulled Lexi aside and ushered the ladies to chairs near where I was seated so I could keep some distance between the dog and our new guests.

It wasn't long before Lexi had edged her way over to the lady who was not a dog person. Before I realized it, Lexi had her head on the leg of the guest. At first, the guest didn't move, reminding us again that she was not a dog person. As she talked, Lexi only looked up at her with her soft, dark-brown eyes, never moving her head from the lady's lap. In only a few moments, the lady looked down at Lexi's big eyes looking back up at her and said she didn't like dogs, but she could learn to like this one. The petting soon followed. Ice had been broken with a gentle touch from Lexi.

I had never been much of a hugger. It wasn't something we did much in our family growing up. We had a lot of love, but not much hugging. Now, we have found value in that touch. We find comfort, peace, appreciation, encouragement, and love for each other with a warm hug. It is amazing how much tension can be drained out of your body in times of stress when a big black or yellow dog comes up to you, puts her head on your lap, and looks up at you with melting eyes.

Maybe that is why so many nursing homes enjoy visits from well-mannered companion dogs. The lonely elderly, who don't get that many visitors, remember a loving touch. "Hug me. I think you need a hug. I know I do."

Don't tell me God doesn't smile when He sees that. I wouldn't be surprised if someday He tells us that He sent us that hug. "It looked like you needed it."

I'm a hugger now.

Sadie mentoring puppy Bella

Walking to Know You More

Looking back on the blessings of our four Labs, it became apparent that the more time we spent with each of those dogs, the better they were. They knew us better and we knew them better. There was a special connection with Boo and then with Lexi, the latest of our family members. The dogs could read our moods and we could read theirs because we spent more time with them.

Three of our dogs were especially adept at picking up when someone was a little down. They would offer a wet kiss, sit particularly close, or just lie down at someone's feet. If you were happy, they were happy. If you were excited, well, anything on the coffee or end tables might require attention if you hoped to save it from the likely crash. A Labrador's tail is the perfect height for those tables. Picture a rapidly swinging broomstick with hair, and you pretty much have a Lab's tail down. A happy Lab tail can bruise legs and clean tables in ready fashion.

Dogs are very seldom in a down mood—or at least one that lasts very long. They live in the moment. Whatever is happening in the present moment can erase whatever happened ten or fifteen minutes earlier. We can learn from their short-term memory when it comes to problems. They can dismiss a mistake—and learn from it—but not let the misstep continually be a drag on them. It is the same as God's forgiveness of our sins. When we ask for forgiveness and repent, God forgets our transgressions or rebellious acts and removes them as far as the east is from the west (Psa. 103:12). That is forever. He doesn't dwell on our mistakes—and neither should we. We'd do well to learn a dog's ten-minute rule in that regard—learn from our errors and move on.

With Boo, my wife was at home all day once we started our family. Tim and Mandy grew up with that dog always around. Boo went on long trips with us, went camping with us, and went to the store with us. Where we went, she almost always went, too. She knew us well and we knew her well.

I once wrote a tongue-in-cheek newspaper column about training this dog with extra-sensory-perception (ESP). I had read about a woman who thought animals had special ESP abilities. The idea made me wonder about the possibilities. Wouldn't it be cool to just think a command and have your dog respond? You could really impress your friends; maybe win a few friendly wagers. Of course, there also was the vast saving of energy required of verbal commands. I wouldn't even have to lift my hand to point. It would be so cool.

I figured Boo was around us so much that she could read our minds. I wrote how I tried to get her to come to me just by thinking it with intensity. That would be the ESP. I really concentrated on the command. All it did was give me a headache. Boo was napping. But when I gave up and decided to get an iced tea from the fridge, there she was at my side to see if there was something in there she might get to share. So much for ESP. I reasoned all one had to do was train a dog by somehow using the sound of opening a refrigerator door. Yes, I knew my dog well.

With Pepper and Sadie, my wife and I worked more hours away from the home. I had changed jobs, and my wife had returned to the workforce. The kids were in school, so the only time we spent with those dogs was mornings, evenings, and weekends. Somebody would try to get home for lunch to let them out, but it didn't always happen. They were very good dogs, mind you, but there was just a little missing connection. They didn't get the amount of quality time Boo had enjoyed.

Most of our friends knew Sadie and thought she was terrific. She indeed was special, but they didn't get to meet Boo. Boo was off the charts on good-dog scales, which I attribute to her good breeding and our time together.

Lexi is getting the benefit of my having much more flextime in my job and of my decision to take her for frequent car rides. She also was allowed to come to work with me on occasion as a pup, which seemed to delight my coworkers. It sure was fun for me, too, and offered much more training time. Lexi had such a great personality, much like Boo, and loved being around people, especially children. It was a unique office environment that allowed one of the single moms to also bring her son to the office often. He and Lexi would play for hours. It was good for both of them. He would challenge her to learn new tricks, and I challenged him to help her learn to do more.

Boo benefited from extra bonding time, as Lexi did. They learned to know us better because of the effort we made to invest the time with them. It helped them become even better dogs. Lexi is on track to become the best one yet, largely because of the bonding time. My wife calls her my shadow. She might as well be attached to my hip when I am at home, but that is a good place for both of us.

The bond has been so close with most of my dogs that they want even more time together. If you are in the vicinity, they want to be with you. They could be in a deep sleep, but if I moved to another room in the house, in a matter of minutes, my dogs would come looking for me. When a family member is home, Boo and Lexi were and are seemingly only content to take a nap in the room with that family member. They are uneasy and restless when the bond of proximity is broken. If you left the house, the dogs would wait at the window, watching for your return. If you were home, they would try to seek you out to stay in touch. They were and are comforted in the connection.

It also has dawned on me that when we make a serious effort to bond with God we become even better at knowing Him and His will for us. That shouldn't be surprising to most people, but the revelation came to me a little later in life. Many people have hinted to me that it is called maturing. In truthful self-evaluation, I'll go along with that. I find the more I know, the more I want to know. I have a hunger for connection. I find comfort in the closeness of the bond.

I have had several challenging bosses over the years. I jokingly referred to them as "evil" bosses—okay, maybe only half in jest. The one thing the first of those bosses did for me was push me closer to my Bible. He didn't know it, of course, nor would he have ever recommended it. The intense pressure at work created a lot of stress. It kept me up at night. My head hurt. My stomach hurt. I believe it was probably my wife who suggested I find answers and rest in the Bible. I began reading it each night after coming home from working the late shift. It was the only comfort I could get to help me go to sleep after receiving many unkind and often unjustified assessments of my hardworking and honest efforts in a tough job. I did strive for perfection, but I just wasn't perfect.

My nightly reading of God's word gave me a peace that surpassed understanding. Go figure—God's own word says that will happen. If you do this, you will experience God's peace, which is far more wonderful than the human mind can understand. His peace will guard your hearts and minds as you live in Christ Jesus (New Living Translation, Phil. 4:7). I don't know exactly how or why, but I started sleeping quite well. I was anxious to go to work. Much of work was fun, and my coworkers were wonderful for the most part.

God ingrained in my mind a verse in Romans (8:31): "If God is for me, who can be against me," It gave me strength to persevere. King David mentioned it in several of his Psalms, reminding himself of God's awesome power and protection in the face of David's own evil boss—King Saul. Saul, at that point, was trying to hunt David down to kill him. God provided David's protection. David grew to have great trust in God for that protection.

I found new strength, new knowledge, and even comfort in being closer to God. The more time I spent in His word, the more I knew Him. The more I knew Him, the more fervent I became in my pursuit to become a better Christian in my daily walk. I began to realize I needed to be the best man I could be, not just best husband or best employee. I was working first for God, and His standards are pretty high.

I started to understand the steps He desired for me to take, even in adversity. More importantly, I realized He was attached to *my* hip. He was with me all the time, through my good and bad days. If, for some reason, I felt He had abandoned me, it was I who moved, *not* He. I left the house. He waits at the window. He desires us to seek Him out on those occasions and return home to Him. There is peace and comfort at home in His arms. I can find rest curled up at the feet of His throne.

During my eight years as an outdoor writer, Boo and I made a lot of trips to the field. Most often it was for hunting. She loved to hunt, loved to retrieve, and was really special when it came to finding any birds those in our hunting party may have knocked down. Many of my hunting partners also had their own dogs, but Boo made most of the retrieves. I loved to watch that dog work. As the years passed, I really began to enjoy watching that dog work more than the hunt itself.

She was a natural. She had a great nose and instinctively knew birds were something the master sought. She would go find him some. When she was just four or five months old, we would go to the field, where I practiced zigzagging through the high grass. I would let her run ahead of me, but would call her back if she ventured too far. I would whistle when I changed direction. She would look back, and I would wave my arm in the new way she was to go. I added a voice command of "right" or "left," and she soon picked up on that. It proved to be a wonderful set of commands when trying to position her later in our hunting adventures. Yes, this was going to be a pretty special puppy.

One calm and clear spring day, I decided to head out to south-central Nebraska's marshlands to take a few pictures and write a story about the waterfowl migration. Back then, springtime in Nebraska had no waterfowl-hunting season, but I didn't want to go for a hunt anyway, at least not with a shotgun. I was hunting with my camera. My idea was to see the ducks and geese that came through the region during their migration to northern nesting areas.

It should be noted that central Nebraska is famous in the wildlife world as a staging area for the annual migration of the sandhill crane. The vast majority of sandhill cranes in North America funnel through central Nebraska each spring. It is a spectacle, a wonder of nature that draws thousands of people to witness it each year.

Much attention has always been given to the cranes in the spring, but it is almost forgotten that thousands of other waterfowl species also migrate through Nebraska. Those were the birds I wanted to see, the colorful ducks and geese that filled the wetlands south of the central Platte River. The spring plumage of those ducks, in particular, is really impressive. The males of the species put on their best colors for the mating season to soon arrive. I wanted to collect a few more pictures of these birds in full bloom.

I stopped just before lunchtime to grab a couple of hamburgers at a fast-food restaurant and then drove to a quiet marsh. I could see thousands of ducks and geese circling, setting their wings, and "snow-flaking," as I called it, to the open waters below. It is one of my favorite things to watch in the wild. The instinctive ability of those birds is impressive to see as they stretch out their wings, then rock gently back and forth, allowing the wind beneath their wings to help them settle to a soft landing in the marsh waters. It is like watching large flakes of snow gently rocking as they fall to cover the ground on a windless day.

I spotted a small dike running into the marsh and a little cedar tree growing in the middle of the dike. I grabbed the lunch, my camera, and a blanket to sit on. Boo and I walked slowly out to the tree, which would help break our silhouette against the sky. I hoped the tree would hide us slightly. Our arrival didn't seem to bother the birds much. They kept coming and going. It was a phenomenal scene, very similar to a Terry Redlin painting, *Best Friends,* which I saw many years later. The gifted artist captured the scene of that special moment so well that a copy of the painting graces a wall in our home. Somebody else had found the same pleasure in watching the marsh and the abundant life in flight it drew.

The true beauty of that day, however, with my special dog at my side, was the marvel of God's creation and greatness. I often was struck by the wonder of God when sitting next to a free-flowing river or visiting the mountains. The scenery and tranquility of those natural settings brings a peace to you. You are right with the world in those moments. I held those visions and the memory of that feeling while reading my nightly Bible verses many years later. It is one of those feelings to long for always.

The day in the marsh hit me with a similar special appreciation for the Creator. God really makes great things. He paints with a brush that fills your eyes and mind with colors and beauty that simply take the rest of the world away for at least a while. The troubles of your life melt away. You can sit there and talk with your dog, and with God. God's gentle breeze is soothing and comforting. Maybe that was the gentle whisper Elijah experienced in 1 Kings 19:11–12 when waiting for God to show up:

> "Go out and stand before me on the mountain," the Lord told him. And as Elijah stood there, the Lord passed by, and a mighty windstorm hit the mountain. It was such a terrible blast that the rocks were torn loose, but the Lord was not in the wind. After the wind, there was an earthquake, but the Lord was not in the earthquake. And after the earthquake, there was a fire, but the Lord was not in the fire. And after the fire there was the sound of a gentle whisper.

God showed up.

I sensed Boo felt God's closeness, too. As much as she loved retrieving birds, she just sat there with me, watching. I never had to say a word to her to stay with me. This was a hunting dog, a hunting machine, but there was no quivering in anticipation, no whimpering to be sent after the birds. There was not even panting that dogs often do when they are excited or anxious. She didn't lie down. She just sat and watched. Maybe the ESP thing was taking hold, sensing my peace. I think it was more likely she just enjoyed the view as much as I did. For nearly two hours, we just sat and marveled at the grace and beauty of those birds coming and going in the marsh. Life in that moment was pretty special. God's great creation was on display. Boo and I drew it in as best we could. God was in that place, and He felt very close.

Proverbs 8:17 says, "I love those who love Me, and those who seek Me, find Me." When we go searching, He shows us He is there. When we know He is there, life just seems better through the highs and even the lows. It is times like that when all is well, yet you wonder why there are bad times. Why can't life be this tranquil all the time? Why are there bumps in the road of life? Couldn't God just flip a switch and make everything good, smooth, and harmonious?

The answer, of course, is yes. If He is the almighty, all-powerful God that I believe Him to be, He could do that. And I believe the day is coming when He will. Until that day, however, we have to deal with the bumps, but we can learn from them.

The Bible doesn't tell us that when we become Christians, all our trials and tribulations go away. Honestly, it tells us we are likely to have trials and tribulations if we are to mirror Christ in our walk. So then, since Christ suffered physical pain, you must arm yourselves with the same attitude he had and be ready to suffer too (1 Pet. 4).

Those trials and tests are actually good for us. They help us mature in our walk. They help us understand life the way God wants us to see it. Sometimes I believe He heats us up to get our attention, to help us improve, and to draw us nearer to Him. It is the image of the refiner's fire for making pure gold. God will heat up our lives at times as the refiner heats gold. However, heating gold too much reportedly will ruin it. It is heated just enough to separate some of the impurities from the precious metal, and then it is heated again to do more of the same. Eventually there will be pure gold—so pure it is almost mirror-like.

> These trials are only to test your faith, to show that it is strong and pure. It is being tested as fire tests and purifies gold—and your faith is far more precious to God than mere gold. So if your faith remains strong after being tried by fiery trials, it will bring you much praise and glory and honor on the day when Jesus Christ is revealed to the whole world (1 Pet. 1:7).

I believe God heats us with tests in our lives so He can show us some of our impurities that need to be removed. He doesn't heat us to a level that we can't handle. Eventually, He will make us pure, so pure we can reflect Him through our hearts and actions toward others. The heating, tests, and trials aren't enjoyable. Many are painful, and some are frightening in our walk through this life. The difference is that as

God-loving, God-fearing Christians we never have to walk alone. He promises to be with us on the walk.

As the Israelites ended their forty-year wandering in the wilderness, God directed Moses to tell the people to have comfort in the challenges ahead because He was walking with them. They could stand strong and prevail, even against giants in the land. Deuteronomy 31:6 says, "Be strong and courageous. Do not be afraid or terrified because of them, for the Lord your God goes with you; He will never leave you nor forsake you." We are comforted in the connection. The psalmist had it right in Psalm 23:4. "Though I walk through the valley of the shadow of death, I will fear no evil for you are with me …"

Walk with me. Let me get to know you more. God is a God of relations, too. Boo and I felt His presence in the marsh. It felt strongly as if God was walking with us that day, sitting with us in the marsh. He came in the whisper of the wind. It was a very good day.

Boo at guard for baby Mandy

Walking with Angels

There are times in life when we just don't feel safe. Maybe you are aware of a challenge on your path ahead. You might have to walk in a neighborhood that is dark and scary. Those are times you can benefit from having a supporting partner, someone or something to give you a boost of confidence. It is helpful to have that someone assure you life is okay. You will make it through this test.

On more than one occasion, I have found that assurance in my dogs. On several other occasions, I only wished I had one of my dogs with me when I walked through one of those fearful valleys. I have uttered more than a few prayers for protection in those instances, and I knew God would be with me, but I sure would have loved to have Him send along one of the dogs, too.

I think dogs may well be God's guardian angels in the flesh. I learned to trust them and their judgment. Boo was the ultimate guardian. During my sports writing career, I covered a lot of football, basketball, and baseball games. One night after covering a high school basketball game, I drove home, patted the dog on the head when she greeted me at the door, and quickly headed to bed. The game had gone into three overtimes. It was very late by the time I filed my final story. I was mentally wiped out. Once home and in bed I must have fallen asleep quickly and deeply.

It seemed as if only minutes later when the doorbell rang. Boo, sleeping on the floor next to me, let out a couple of deep warning barks.

She was a very big girl by then, standing above my knee and weighing nearly ninety pounds. She was all muscle. I was startled from my deep sleep, jumped up, and looked out the window near the bed to see several police cars lining the street in front of the house. I wondered if I had hit someone in my mentally diminished condition on the drive home from the ballgame. Maybe I had driven through a stop sign. I was very tired, so I tried not to speed home, but this was like one of those high-speed chase scenarios where every patrol car in a given county shows up to assist.

My mind was racing over what might be wrong as I tugged on some jeans and a T-shirt and headed to the door. I opened it to see one of the officers on my porch and several in the yard. The officer on the porch said, "Please don't worry. We are raiding one of the houses behind you. We suspect one of the young men back there is selling drugs. If you hear some noise, it's us. We just wanted you to know so you wouldn't be frightened."

While it made me wonder about what our quiet neighborhood had become, the comment did give me some peace that I had not done anything wrong. Just as I started to relax a bit, I heard a deep growl and looked down to see Boo crouching to leap at the man who had made me feel uncomfortable. I reached down and caught her collar just as she hit the screened door. The officer backed up quickly with rather large eyes and said, "Oh, and please keep the dog inside." Yep, I felt safe, and it wasn't because of the police presence.

When we had our first child, people warned us to be careful with a big dog in the house. You never know if the new baby could trigger jealousy in the dog. That first day home, I took our son Tim and began rocking him. I called Boo over and told her this was her new boy. She was to watch him carefully. She smelled him and licked his foot. She then curled up on the floor next to the rocker. She was signaling that she was okay with this new little person in the house. There would be no jealousy at all.

Without prodding, Boo slept under Tim's crib for the first three nights he was home. We thought it was a little strange since she had never slept anywhere but on or next to our bed in the other bedroom.

We soon found out how truly accepting she was of this newest member of her pack. Nobody could go look in on Tim without Mom or Dad being there. Even my own mother experienced something new about this dog she had grown to know and like. Mom was so anxious to come see her new grandbaby that she didn't heed a word of warning when she came to visit a day after Tim came home from the hospital. She bolted right for the baby's room. Boo came quickly out from under the crib and backed her out of the room with a low growl and a showing of hair and teeth. Mom recalled that story to Tim more than thirty years later. Boo had made an impression on her that day. Her new grandbaby had a personal guardian angel. Boo hadn't gotten the word that grandmothers were okay to visit her boy.

Yes, we had to watch our big dog all right, but for the safety of anybody who might be messing with Tim. She took my words to heart. She watched him carefully.

When we had our second child, Mandy, Boo adopted her just as quickly. Mandy liked to play in the backyard in her playpen under our big shade tree. Boo's place generally was right next to the playpen. Just as with Tim, Boo would check out anybody who came near the baby.

One afternoon, a neighbor was babysitting the kids and letting them play in our fenced yard. We had gone to a couples' event that afternoon. Not long after that, we were called to the phone. It was the babysitter. She said she was watching the children playing in the yard, but was concerned. There was a car parked just down the street and a man inside was watching them rather suspiciously.

There had been reports in previous weeks of child abductions and molestations in our city and the police had warned everyone to be on alert. The young sitter was worried.

I asked, "Where's Boo?"

The sitter said she had left her in the house. I told her to take the dog outside and to tell me what happened next. Sure enough, Boo went out and took her normal spot next to Mandy's playpen. The sitter started to chuckle with relief on the phone. The car was leaving. I asked whether she had learned anything.

She said, "Don't mess with these kids. They've got a big guard dog, and she's always going to be with us from now on."

Boo was the supreme example of a dog watching over us. She was the kids' constant companion, their pillow, and personal vacuum cleaner at meal or snack time. I never worried for the family when she was around. She was very gentle with the kids, but was big enough to be quite intimidating. Strangers would be met with a big bark that told them they might want to think about what they did next, and it probably should not be anything threatening.

Nearly a year after Tim was born, my wife started receiving threatening and suggestive phone calls every time I went away on a writing assignment. Boo regularly went with me. That would leave my wife and young son home alone. With the threats, however, I decided the guard dog would start staying home. I had confidence that Boo would have sacrificed her life to protect any one of us. Whoever might try to cross the line with one of us would have to answer to her, and that would be a very bad choice. She was a walking muscle. Fortunately, the authorities tracked down the suspect before the dog was tested. No more calls.

Boo's strength was surprising to me on more than one occasion. In those days before micro-chipping your dogs, I took her to get an identification tattoo offered by the Humane Society. The Humane Society offered tattooing as a special event in one of the city parks. Anybody was welcome to bring a family pet for a permanent identification. The operation had two very big men helping the young lady who had the tattoo device. The men would hold the dog down until the lady was done. Boo and I followed a Saint Bernard in the line of people and their pets. I was curious to see how the really big dog did with all the commotion. The men seemed to handle the Saint Bernard comfortably. I had to help them hold Boo down. This was one strong dog.

In another example of a guardian angel, my wife was home with baby Tim one afternoon when she heard a muffled cry for help coming from our basement. She opened the basement door and saw a utility meter reader pinned against the basement wall. Boo was just a few feet away, showing a lot of raised hair and sharp teeth. She also was offering a low growl, which meant she was very serious. The man couldn't move.

While Boo stayed in position and growled any time the man tried to move, my wife asked him what he was doing in our house. He said he had knocked to get in because he really needed to read our electric meter. When no one answered, he tried the door and let himself in to read the meter. My wife asked if he really thought that big animal in front of him would not have warned her if anyone had knocked on the door. He admitted the dog probably would have barked. Then my wife offered a warning. If the man ever tried that trick again, she would let the dog have at him. Then she called Boo by name and the dog backed off. The man scurried outside with another apology. I'm not sure if he kept his job after his little trick, but Boo never let a meter man so much as jump over the fence after that. It was a trusting time when most people didn't lock their houses or cars. Life was pretty safe overall. Still, things happened at unexpected times. It was good to have a big dog.

Boo was amazingly protective, as I firmly believe God is as well. He is a really big God. He wraps us up in His arms of protection, which is enough, but He also gives us four-legged security for our comfort.

We called Sadie "Mandy's date dog." Sadie wouldn't let anybody hug without getting in the middle of it. Sometimes it was because she wanted in on the hug. Other times, we weren't quite as certain. She wanted a little separation between people if the hugs were too long or too intense. Sometimes we would play with that, hugging each other and one of the parties might fake a scream or act as if they were trying to break out of the grip.

Sadie would jump up on us, trying to wedge in the middle. Sometimes she might even put her mouth gently on an arm and growl softly, as if to warn, "That's enough, unless you want to lose this."

As a dad with a great-looking teenage daughter, I especially loved Sadie at that time in our lives. My wife and I could go to bed when Mandy and one of her boyfriends were still watching television in the family room. We could be assured they were going to behave. Sadie had to stay out there with Mandy. Mandy knew what that meant. The boyfriends soon learned, too.

I once had a security company representative try to sell me a home alarm system. I told him I had one. He asked which brand. I said the big-bodied, four-legged, sharp-teethed brand. He said a dog couldn't really protect our property properly. I told him to talk with my brother-in-law. He came for a visit, knew our dog, and had a key to the house. We were not expected home for a while, but I told him to let himself in and make himself comfortable until we could get there. I found him an hour after his arrival, still standing outside the opened front door. Sadie was at the top of the steps—all hair and teeth. My brother-in-law was not going in without a member of the family giving her the "all clear."

Sadie—like Boo, Pepper, and Lexi—had an amazing, natural guard dog mode. It is something I have encouraged. I ask the dogs to be a guard dog. When somebody approaches the house, I want a "big-girl" bark. You'd be surprised how many door-to-door sales interruptions those barks will deter. Not many would-be burglars would want to take a chance on trying to negotiate with a big dog protecting a house. There are plenty of other easier targets out there.

However, protective angels on four-legs don't have to be big. Our neighbor's sister had a smaller breed of dog. When the woman was attacked by a stranger in her home, the little dog went after the attacker and distracted him enough to allow her to escape. The little dog had no fear when it was his master in trouble. The dog was willing to put his life on the line to protect her.

A young boy in eastern Nebraska found his Lab to be a guardian angel, too. The family regularly camped along the Platte River, which generally is shallow and tranquil. Most people can easily wade across the Platte in many locations because its current is often slow and unthreatening. However, on this particular weekend, a big rainstorm upstream brought a lot of water down the river. When the boy went to play along the shore, he slipped and was swept out into the fast-moving current. The family didn't hear his cries for help, but the family's four-year-old Lab did. He ran to the river, jumped in, and swam to the boy. He grabbed the big dog's collar and the dog swam them both to safety.

We had friends who adopted one of Sadie's puppies. We had one yellow male pup left from her one and only litter. These folks had two kids, and the dad thought it would be great to have a dog for the children. We offered the pup to him. His wife wasn't a dog person and had never been around big dogs. She wasn't excited about how big the pup grew, but the pup was a close companion for her.

One day, the dog came excitedly barking to the wife, who told the dog to wait until she had finished her project. She figured he had to go outside to go to the bathroom. When the dog refused to settle down, the wife said in frustration, "What do you want?" The dog ran to the front door, then came back to her, barked, and returned to the door. She went to the door, looked outside, and saw her young daughter. The girl had been playing with a rope around the tree. She had somehow gotten tangled in the rope and was dangerously close to hanging herself. The dog brought the mom to the rescue.

When Mandy bought her first home in an older neighborhood in our city, she wanted her own Labrador for her guard dog. We found Bella at a local kennel. This little black puppy grew to be a great companion for Mandy. One night, Mandy heard noises outside her home. Bella was quietly growling to tip Mandy there was something—or someone—out there. When she heard footsteps on her porch, the dog let go with her warning barks in big-girl mode. They were followed by sounds of someone running off.

While Mandy and her mother were uncomfortable about the situation, Mandy felt she had a protector in her dog. She told me she liked the thought of a black Lab because if threatening people came around in the dark, they might hear Bella, but they wouldn't see her coming until it was too late. I knew the police officer on my porch those many years earlier was thinking the same thing about Boo.

Our loving dogs can—and often do—put it all on the line for us. They can find us when we are lost. They can lead us or pull us to safety. They have been known to detect cancer in a person, sense when a person is about to have a seizure, or belly-crawl in to help a wounded soldier.

I had no doubt Boo would have taken on the police officer on my front porch that night. I had no doubt—as shy as Pepper was, as loving as Sadie was, or as gentle as Lexi is—that those dogs would come to our rescue in a time of need. To put their lives on the line for us is a self-sacrificing, agape-type love—the ultimate kind.

I pray almost daily for God to wrap us up in His arms of protection. When I think of my loving guard dogs, I smile. God loves us enough to send the very best.

Smiling Sparky with Georgie

Walking in Joy

There is something infectious about a person whose life in the moment is bubbling over with joy. They are smiling, giggling, laughing loudly, squirming, hugging everybody, or doing a happy dance. If you are really happy, it is hard to sit still. It is great to personally be in those moments, or even to watch someone else in one. I bet the thought of such a happy person is bringing a smile to your face as you read this. You know what I mean. Those ecstatically joyful experiences seem to come along way too seldom for those of us who are mired in today's busy, workaholic world. Young children seem to have more of those moments, largely, I suspect, because they have not yet been tainted by the world. For adults, way too infrequently do we bubble up in happy times—unless you have a little bit of joyful inoculation waiting for you when you get home.

A dog's welcome home is a great example of pure joy, reminding us what genuine happiness should be and that it should be experienced and shared often.

There is an Internet posting that keeps coming around to me, probably because people know I am a dog person. I chuckle every time I see it because of the truth therein.

There are different versions of it, but it goes something like a dog's outlook on life:

- Going for a ride—my favorite thing.
- Fetching the morning paper—my favorite thing.

- Getting a new chew bone—my favorite thing.
- Having my master pet me—my favorite thing.

The list can go on and on for dogs, but the contrasting outlook on life from a cat is more abbreviated:

- Day 695 of my captivity—still plotting my escape.

I wish we all could have a dog's outlook on life. They are generally happy, full of energy, ready to play, and eager to go for a ride or a walk. They are pleasers. That brings them joy.

Every one of our dogs has expressed an abundance of joy whenever any family member came home or, in a more subdued manner, when we welcomed a guest. You could be gone for fifteen minutes and the greeting was the same when you returned. The dogs are delighted you came back. It is like, "Yeah! You're here. I've missed you so much!" It is an amazing display to see the joy of a dog just to be in your presence again. All of our dogs were quite expressive, but they all showed their joy in different ways.

My first memory of this was with our farm dog, Sparky, a cocker spaniel-border collie cross. Sparky was an outdoor dog, but she and my dad had a morning routine. As soon as she saw my dad come out of the house, she would start running and wagging. She would wag her tail so hard that she would start running sideways. Then she would break out an amazing smile. There was no doubt she was smiling. This was one happy dog. She could not contain her joy. This was her guy—and he was coming out of the house.

Sparky would come skidding to a stop in front of my dad, and he would put his hands on his hips, look down, and say, "Sparky, you're just a dog." It always deflated her. She just crumpled at his feet. "How could this be?" Then he would reach down and pet her. "But you're a really good dog." The smile returned. Sparky had new life. The joy was back. Life was good. The master loves me. I did well.

I wonder whether it was the kind of feeling the two servants had in Jesus's parable of the talents in Matthew. "Well done, my good and faithful servant." Three servants were given a specific amount of money by the master before he departed for a while. One servant received five talents, the second two talents, and a third servant one talent. The one given five had invested it and earned five more. The one with two did likewise, doubling his investment for the master. The one who was given one talent buried it in the yard. It earned nothing because he was afraid of losing it. He thought his master was cruel and hard. Upon his return, the master gave rewards to those servants who did the most with what they were given. They didn't see their master as a mean man. The servant who earned nothing, however, was cast out.

There are some Bible scholars who consider the talents to be our physical or spiritual gifts given us to use for God's glory. To me, that makes a lot of sense. The Apostle Paul wrote to the Corinthians that when we accept Jesus as our Savior and become Christians, we are given a spiritual gift God intends for us to use in the betterment of His spiritual family. Every Christian has such a gift, but we aren't to bury it. We are to use the talents God gives us to bring honor to Him as best we can. The better we use those talents, the more honor for God. If we do it well, it is hoped that when we pass on to the eternal world, we will get a "Well done, my good and faithful servant!" from our heavenly Master.

Sometimes I wonder if God doesn't instill special gifts in other creatures as well. Maybe He sends us another little hint about using our talents instead of burying them.

Sparky had a talent—a spiritual gift—if dogs could have one. It was joy. She used it often and used it well to share her delight about life. She radiated happiness. Her joyful spirit just had to come out. When she smiled and wagged sideways, you just had to smile or laugh at her joy. It was infectious.

Boo was the most laid-back of our Labradors and had a purely joyful disposition. Aside from the puppy-jumping episode with the little neighbor girl, she would show her joy with her massive tail. She could dust all of our coffee tables and end tables at the same time when someone came home. We never had to childproof our house for those low items young children could reach. Boo ensured that we had nothing breakable—or even unbreakable—at that height. If there ever was, it wasn't there for long.

When Sadie was young, she would go off into something we called the "puppy spasm." It was as if something internal went off when someone came home or came to visit. She became so happy she couldn't contain herself. The joy in her cup of life was overflowing. She had to let it out. She would drop her tail between her hind legs, pin her ears back, and take off. The layout of our house made for a circle through the rooms, and she could cover it with lightning speed. You couldn't help but share her joy. When you arrived home, your mood didn't matter much because it was going to be lifted in a matter of minutes. Two or three loops were all Sadie usually performed before settling down for "pet-me" time.

I had to learn to just stand still and bend over slightly, putting my two hands out in front of me. It was a signal that this was where the dogs had to settle to receive my "glad-to-see-you" petting. Sadie would spin for a bit in front of you and then settle in between the hands to take it all in. Later in life, when arthritis made it hard for her to bounce and spin, she would simply come up to me and pin her ears back in her "I'm too cute not to love" pose and await her "pet-me" time.

Pepper was a spinner. She just did circles until the initial rush had passed.

Mandy's Bella does something of a happy dance, prancing and waving her thick tail like crazy.

Lexi can stop bouncing for only so long. She is still a puppy at heart at the time of this writing. She is three years old and still has trouble sitting when it comes to greeting a member of the family on a return home. There is too much joy there. She has to launch—straight up. Her vertical jump is really quite something. Her eyes can be level with my eyes, and I stand five-foot-ten. I learned to bend over slightly because the joyful launch could easily blow the glasses right off my nose. Boo could jump, but not like this. We've learned Lexi must be ignored for a minute or two when we first come home. It is hard on her—and us—but soon enough, the bonding rekindles the happy fire burning inside her. The joy bubbles over. She almost quivers in anticipation. When it appears she has settled enough not to go vertical, we can bend over to give her a loving pet. She spins through our hands so we can touch the entire length of her. She is so happy we are home, and she makes us happy we are in her presence, too.

Joy is a good thing. Happy people are healthier people—and a lot more enjoyable to be around. I believe God wants us to be happy. I wonder if He smiles when we are filled with joy. I wonder if He sent us our good dogs to deflate the stress balloons that seemed to keep getting bigger and bigger during our busy days. A happy greeting will do a lot of deflating when we come home.

The prophet Isaiah talks about another homecoming in the Old Testament. He foretells of the day when God will bring His people home.

> Those who have been ransomed by the Lord will return to Jerusalem, singing songs of everlasting joy. Sorrow and mourning will disappear, and they will be overcome with joy and gladness (Isa. 35:10).

There is a vision of the joy of the Lord being with the people. King David danced before the Ark of the Covenant upon its return from captivity. He experienced the joy of the Lord. It was a happy dance. He couldn't sit still.

Do you think we will show as much joy as our dogs when we come into the presence of our heavenly Master, when we finally see Him face to face in the end time? I certainly hope so. I want to be smiling and wagging myself sideways. I want to be so filled with joy that I have an urge for a "puppy spasm" or a happy dance. I want to have trouble sitting because of too much joy. Most of all, I want the Master to pat me on the head and say, "Well done."

Boo at the open gate

Walking the Talk

I had been training dogs for more than thirty years and had three really great Labs previous to our latest experience, but I am by no means a professional-level dog trainer. There are a lot of things I don't know about training. Still, my dogs have always been good, obedient, and loyal. I read several training books and talked with a variety of professional dog trainers about techniques I tried to apply while grooming Boo, Pepper, and Sadie.

One particular dog trainer I interviewed for a story more than thirty years ago was a most-impressive fellow. He had trained seven national field champions, specializing in Brittany Spaniels. One thing he said, however, made a big impression. He said that most people get only 10 percent of the potential out of their dogs. He believed dogs, by and large, were far more intelligent and capable of far more than we give them credit.

In my educated—yet amateurish—way, I tried to train my dogs to be functional at home as well as in the field. Most people told us they were impressed with our Labs. They weren't all perfect, but any one of them could have been readily adopted by a number of people who knew them. I had a couple of people offer me very impressive money to sell them Boo. I told them it would have been like selling one of our kids. It wasn't going to happen.

When Lexi came along, I decided, for the fun of it, to take a puppy-training class through the local Humane Society. It was my first class under someone trained to train the dog trainer. It opened my eyes to something I knew before but never really thought about in my previous puppy training. My new puppy didn't know my language. What a revelation! My little light went on. Of course she didn't know much of anything. Lexi was new to everything. I realized that if I was to raise a truly super dog, I needed to help my little flurry baby learn the language—my language.

In this time of mental enlightenment, I recalled how difficult it had been to learn a new language when I was in the military more than thirty years earlier. I was stationed in Germany, didn't know the local lingo, and had difficulty expressing myself. I had studied Spanish in high school and college, but hadn't learned it very well. It certainly didn't do much good in Germany. I learned a few of the basic German terms, but had to use a form of sign language to communicate with my landlord, who spoke no English. Fortunately, I didn't have to know all the words to get my message across in a way the landlord could understand.

I made mistakes along the way in translation, but with just one exception, the natives found a lot of humor in my efforts. That exception could have been a problem had it not been for some friends of an inebriated man. They saw the humor in my flawed translation of something I thought was totally innocent, but apparently wasn't. They ushered their friend on down the street.

Yes, knowing the language makes life a lot easier for everybody.

In Lexi's training, I thought about how wonderful it would be to have verbal commands and a matching set of hand signals for my puppy. She could see very well so maybe she could pick up hand signals as quickly as verbal commands.

My other dogs had learned a few hand signs, which served us well when we needed to quietly get them to stop bugging visitors.

Boo was very good at responding to hand signs. When we were hunting, all I had to do was wave at her to go in a particular direction and she went. It was great when I had to try to direct her in a brushy creek bed while hunting or to try to find something I wanted her to fetch in the yard.

Boo also learned that if I snapped my fingers and pointed at her when we had visitors at home, she quit what she was doing and came over to lie down at my feet. What a great dog. It wasn't ESP, but it was close to reading my mind.

Pepper was less responsive, but was still a good dog. Sadie took well to our few hand signals. I have always used a snap of the fingers as my attention-getter for the dogs. When they hear me snap my fingers, they looked at me and I could give them a sign to come or lie down.

When Bella had a litter, Mandy and I started training several of the puppies as soon as they started showing an ability to learn. One of those was Lexi. At five or six weeks of age, the pups figured that Mandy coming into the yard usually meant food, water, new toys to chew on, or loving snuggles. They would surround her immediately, simply delighted to see her and enjoy whatever she had brought. Of course, walking would become difficult because several pups would have latched on to her shoelaces. Puppies are always fascinated with shoelaces.

Mandy kenneled the pups overnight in her basement or garage, but they were escape artists from the high-walled birthing box in which they spent their first several weeks. She had to move them to an extra-large wire kennel for their safety—and to save her home from ten potential mischief-makers. When she let the pups out the first thing in the morning—and anytime thereafter—she would tell them to "go in the yard" and then lead them to the backyard. It didn't take many of those trips for them to pick up the command and conduct their own puppy parade to the backyard. The pups were ready for some preschool training.

Mandy decided it would be a great idea to take pictures of our early puppy training to make a little training manual for prospective new pup owners. Since she is a graphic artist, she only needed to insert some photos into the booklet. The booklet was a nice touch to go with the American Kennel Club pedigree paperwork and generational charts to show the new owners the puppies' championship bloodlines.

I was the photographer while Mandy served as instructor as she encouraged the pups to perform training basics: sitting, lying down, not biting, and so on. Repeating the commands regularly during the short sessions brought the lessons home quickly. Puppies are like kindergarten or preschool kids. They can learn, but their attention span is short. They are better students when you can separate them from the class to work on your lessons one-on-one. There are fewer distractions.

The ten pups proved to be more than a handful for Mandy—and for Bella. Once the youngsters were on mushy puppy chow and all but weaned from Bella, I took five of the pups to my house. It was a chance to work and play with two of the little girls we expected to keep in the family. I selected Lexi, a nearly white-blonde girl to replace Sadie, who had been gone for several months. Tim wanted a black female and Bella had only one in her litter—a girl we named Gabbie.

Even while separated from their many siblings, Gabbie and Lexi proved to be a continual frustration if I tried to do any training when they were together. Both pups were very smart. One would perform a command quickly and get a treat. The other then would pounce on her sister to try to snatch the treat or to punish her for doing the trick first. Interestingly, one would pick up some commands quicker than others. One might sit promptly while the other laid down first when hearing or seeing the same command. Seldom would they both do one command in unison. I personally think they made pouncing a game. I eventually had to separate them for any serious training. Besides, I would be laughing too hard at the pouncing puppies to stay serious for very long.

Once the pups learned the language, training became a breeze—even in tandem for Lexi and Gabbie. We coupled hand signals with most every command. Snapping our fingers or making a throat-clearing noise was the attention-getter. To establish that, we followed the new noise with a treat when the pup came to see why we had made the sound. A half-dozen treats were all we needed for the drill. Snapping fingers or clearing our throats thereafter got their attention. Following that with a hand signal or voice command also worked well.

Lexi also has learned to tell me "yes" when I ask her something. One little command means to whisper and I liked it a lot. Mandy taught Bella that one with a finger to the lips, like when her mom didn't want her to use her outside voice inside. Lexi gives a quiet woof as her "yes," She is whispering and using her inside voice to confirm her answer. "Do you need to go outside? Are you out of water?" She has learned the language and is communicating back to me. She gives me a whisper and heads to the door, to her water dish, or grabs her snack ball to hand to me to fill.

Lexi also has a "big-girl" voice. I say, "Speak." I cup a hand over my ear, as if to say, "I can't hear you." She increases her volume. Delightfully, that also is her "guard-dog" voice. She is relatively small in stature, but you wouldn't know that by her bark.

As I realized how important it was for the pup to learn the language, the frustration in training I had sometimes experienced with previous pups was all but eliminated. I had more patience. I realized I hadn't learned German in a couple of days either. However, once I knew the pups knew their commands and they didn't perform, then I could correct more firmly so they could learn obedience was expected by the master.

Isn't that just like our growth in our spiritual walk? When we first hear the word about a loving, merciful God who loved us enough to send His Son to die for our sins, we have no idea what that means. We don't know the language of such love. We don't know much about obedience to God. For that matter, we don't know that much about God.

As we begin to grow and mature in the lessons of the Bible and study with others who know, we learn much faster. Having a good mentor helps us as well. It speeds the process even more.

Philippians 3:17 says, "Join with others in following my example, brothers, and take note of those who live according to the pattern we gave you." The Apostle Paul offered himself as a living example, a model, and a mentor for living a Christ-like life. He is a supreme example of the adage: "Witness always and sometimes use words." We learn much by watching one who walks in an exemplary manner. Paul, of course, also used words very well.

As a younger adult, I always figured I could visit with God out in the great outdoors. I know a lot of guys like that. We didn't have to go to church to find God. He was out there with us—like the day in the marsh with Boo. I could sense God's presence. It is very real.

As I matured in my Christian walk—and finally gave in to my wife's prompting to go with her to church—I found an understanding of God I had not previously known. Sure, God is in the great outdoors. He created it. However, really getting to know God, understanding what He wants of us, and seeing how we can bring more glory to Him takes some coaching. We need a good preacher to help us, a Sunday school teacher to take us deeper, and maybe a mentor or two to really help us with the understanding and application to life.

Looking back, I missed so many years of growth and a walk much closer to God by not being in a good Bible-teaching church. I needed a good mentor to help communicate God's message for me earlier in my life. I needed somebody to tell me, educate me, and show me what an obedient life in God was all about. I needed someone to show me what it looked like. I had to learn obedience was not a penalty—it was protection. It was good for me. It was like God putting a fence around me—a fence that didn't restrict me as much as it kept me safe from many hazards in the world. I needed to learn the discipline to stay behind the fence.

That is a good parallel for our walk with God and our walk with dog. A fenced yard allows for some exercise, but it also provides a big measure of protection—at least when we, or our dogs, learn the rules.

I taught my dogs a "stay-in-the-yard" command. It is meant to teach the dogs boundaries they should not cross. The kids, a visitor, or someone might mistakenly leave a gate open. What then? A free-running dog can get into a lot of trouble—or maybe get killed. I didn't want that for them any more than God wants that for me.

Boo was unbelievable with the "stay-in-the-yard" command. Our first home had a big fenced backyard, but the fenced portion was about twenty feet from the back of the house. It was inconvenient to have to walk the dog out to the gate and put her in the fenced yard. The layout of the property also made it nearly impossible to expand the fence to the house so we could just let the dog out the door and know she was within the fencing.

Boo was a great jumper and easily could clear the forty-two-inch fence with her powerful leap. I learned that one day when she came over the top at an inopportune time. I had to pick her up and put her back in the yard after her escape. She didn't like coming off the ground in a manner that was not of her own doing, so she learned staying in the yard meant just what the master said. She would not come out of the yard again without an okay.

She was so delightful and capable of learning. We soon discovered we could let Boo out the back door and tell her to get into the yard. She would go to the gate and jump it to go into the yard. When she was done doing her thing, she would come to the gate and bark. We could open the back door, tell her "okay," and she would jump the gate to come in.

One day, one of the neighbors had errands to run and asked if her young daughters could play with Tim for a while. My wife said it was fine, and the kids headed out to play in the sandbox in the fenced portion of our backyard. Boo went out with them and watched them play for more than an hour. Our neighbor returned with cookies and Kool-Aid as a treat for the kids. The ladies called the kids in and sat them down for their treat.

From elsewhere in the house, I heard Boo bark, which meant she wanted to come in. I asked if somebody had left the dog outside. Our neighbor looked out the kitchen window to see where Boo was; the dog was sitting at the open gate, barking to come in.

"You have got to be kidding," she said. "Come look at this." We looked out to see Boo doing what she was supposed to do. She was staying in the yard. Nobody had told her it was okay to come in. The neighbor couldn't believe the dog was that obedient, so I told her to go to the door and yell, "okay." She did and Boo raced into the house to clean up crumbs from the cookie-munchers. That dog wasn't going anywhere until she had an okay.

Boo was just as good at learning our lot lines, which makes for a really good neighbor. She would go to the end of our property and stop when told to stay in the yard. She would not cross over to the neighbors' property. We could let her out the front door in the morning when the neighbor kids were going to school. She loved it and so did they. She would go to the curb and wait for several children. They would hug her and pet her, and she would walk them down the sidewalk to the end of our lot. She would stop there—and they couldn't coax her to go on. Instead, she would go back and chaperone more kids. Boo was so obedient that it was easy to keep her safe. She learned her limits from me. As her mentor, I wanted her safe, and I set boundaries. As master, I was the lawmaker, but I found out later our dogs could also learn much from having their own four-legged mentor.

Bella was a new puppy when she came to visit one weekend. Sadie really enjoyed the little black pup. Sadie had been a great momma to her own litter many years earlier. With Bella, Sadie was very tolerant—even though Sadie was old and needed the occasional nap without something bouncy tugging at her ears to play. She would let the pup know when Bella had crossed the line.

Bella's learning curve was very impressive. She watched Sadie when I would give a command. It was interesting to see how Bella tried to decipher what this guy was telling the old dog. Bella would cock her head as she listened intently, and then look up at the old dog to see what that meant. I didn't realize just how she translated that until one day when the three of us were outside. It was Bella's first exposure to "stay in the yard," Sadie also was very good at obeying this one.

Sadie was a great mentor for Bella, and the pup learned a lot from the old dog. I was working in the backyard on a project as the two dogs played. I needed something from the garage in front, so I walked through the gate, leaving it open as I went toward the front of the house. Sadie came prancing up as she always did. She wanted to go with me, but I told her to stay in the yard since I'd be right back. She sat at the open gate. Bella was ten weeks old and came bouncing up, too. I repeated the stay-in-the-yard command and held up an open hand. Bella stopped, looked up at Sadie, and—to my surprise—promptly sat down next to the old dog.

I thought that was too good to be true. I walked around the corner of the house, out of sight and fully expected to have a puppy join me at any moment. I waited a little while, and then retrieved what I wanted from the garage. It had been more than five minutes—an eternity in puppy time. I came back around the corner and there at the open gate were my two obedient dogs, old and young. Bella had learned a lot by watching. It was so much easier with a mentor who understood the language.

Mentoring often means living your life and doing your job, but doing it well. Like all my Labs, Sadie always retrieved the morning newspaper from of the driveway. She loved that morning chore and would wait at the door to get the paper—even before she went out to make her morning visit to the grass. She earned a piece of bread for that paper, and she loved bread.

When Bella was nearly nine months old, she came to stay for a week while Mandy went on a trip with friends. Bella raced out with Sadie to get the paper the first morning, but Bella had no clue why the old dog was skipping briskly to the middle of the driveway. Sadie picked up the paper and headed back to the house with Bella bouncing alongside. Sadie took the paper to the kitchen, and I gave both dogs a piece of bread.

The second morning Bella again followed Sadie, now associating going outside with picking something up. She tried to share the burden of the paper with Sadie, but Sadie wasn't sharing. Bella tried to grab hold of the paper, but Sadie would turn her head away and threw a shoulder into Bella to keep the pup away. I didn't hear a growl of warning, but I wouldn't have been surprised if it was offered. Sadie had her job, and she wanted her bread. Off to the kitchen she went. Her treat waited.

On the third morning, Bella, who was much quicker than the old dog, raced to the newspaper and stood on it. She now associated the morning driveway race with the paper. She just didn't know what to do with it. Sadie caught up and actually had to knock the big pup off of the paper to make her daily retrieve. It took a good shoulder bump to get Bella off the paper. It was kind of humorous to watch.

On the fourth morning, Bella raced out to the paper and picked it up. She was about halfway back to the house by the time poor Sadie was halfway down the steps. All Sadie could do was turn and follow Bella to the house. She acted a little down about missing out on the retrieve, but I still rewarded both with some bread.

On the fifth morning, Sadie didn't even go outside. I was amazed. She sat and waited at the door with me. Bella raced out, scooped up the paper, brought it to the door, and dropped it at Sadie's feet. Sadie calmly picked it up and took it into the kitchen as if it was a rehearsed relay. I don't know how dogs really communicate in such a manner, but this was really interesting. Apparently to show it was no fluke, they did it the same way the next day.

This pup had learned something just by watching the old dog's example. The seventh morning was the Sunday paper—and it was a heavy one. The pup bolted from the door. Sadie stayed at my side, but when Bella tried to pick up the paper, it was too much for her. She dropped the end of the bundle when she tried to lift it and headed to the grass as if it was too hard and she was not going to bother. Sadie looked at me, and it was almost as if her mouth dropped open in disbelief. I said, "Well, I guess you have to get this one." Out she went to do her duty. It was easy for her. She knew how to pick up a Sunday paper.

Life with God doesn't necessarily become easier for us, but the walk does, especially when we have someone more mature in the faith to mentor us. We learn the loving Master's words of guidance for our lives. We also learn much about how to apply His words by watching a living example of a Godly life. In some respects, they are the visual hand signals of God's efforts to help us lead better lives. We see evidence of His work in and around us. We come to understand the concept that good comes from obeying. The Master's voice (or written words) can keep us out of trouble, give us comfort, and help us do right. We can learn to sit at the open gate and let the temptations of the world go by. Furthermore, we learn to ask the Master—in total trust—when it is okay to leave the yard. As we grow, we learn to pick up the Sunday paper. Heavier lifting becomes easier when doing what is right through God's word.

There are times God seems to tell me to just sit, wait, don't whimper or whine—watch a good mentor and learn. The proper time to act is not yet at hand. Wait at the gate. Then, at other times, I can almost hear Him yell, "Go get 'em! This is your time."

I have learned to seek His permission and listen for the Master's commands. I am learning His language through my prayer life and Bible reading. I ask for clarity in decision-making, and peace when I have to make a choice in important matters. I don't always get it right. Sometimes the lifting seems pretty heavy when I have to stretch out of my comfort zone, but I'm still learning. I keep getting better the more I practice, the more I trust, and the more I obey.

Through comments from friends and coworkers over the years, I also have found—to my surprise—that I have become a mentor to some of them through the life I live. I find pleasure in my obedience, have been able to stay strong in times of trial, and have learned more about turning from temptations by knowing it is what my Master desires. I just try to do one day at a time—and do it the way God would have me do it. There is a sense of internal satisfaction as a reward when I actually accomplish such a goal on those good days. That is my daily piece of bread.

Mandy training a pup to sit

The Consistent Walk

One thing I have learned about training dogs—and kids for that matter—is that you have to be consistent and you must require them to be consistent in their obedience, too. If you give a command once they understand the language, you must make certain they perform the task. They learn there are no exceptions and no outs. You don't want a sloppy, disobedient dog. It only leads to frustration—possibly years of it.

It is a challenging assignment, but a must to create a super dog for you, your family, and your guests. The dog must know that when the master talks, there are expectations. You expect obedience—and they must learn to respect obedience.

Sometimes training other family members or guests is also necessary for the betterment of your dog. It is all about consistency. Everybody needs to be on the right page to help develop consistent good behavior in the dog.

Consider playing a game where the rules always change. How do you play that? He who makes the rules wins, right? If you aren't making the rules, and the rules are never consistent, what fun is that?

When I was training young Boo, one bit of advice I picked up from some source was to use a rolled up newspaper and swat the pup when it acted improperly. The idea is that the newspaper makes a noise that sounds really horrific, even if the swat is pretty minor in reality. And, again, please understand I didn't beat my dogs. I did try the paper-swatting technique, however. The unfortunate part is that Boo soon determined she didn't have to really mind unless the boss or my wife had a rolled up newspaper. When I assessed that little setback, I changed the rules. There were no more newspapers. The pup quickly determined that if the boss or Mrs. Boss gave a command—newspaper or not—it was better to obey. We had to adapt so the pup knew we really were consistent in what we expected of her.

I ran across a "Pickles" cartoon once that explained consistency quite well in dog terms. The husband scolds his wife with words something like, "How many times have I told you. It is always or never." The wife apologized. She explained that she only did it once. The cartoon strip then shows the dog sitting in a chair, enjoying his own plate of food on the table. The husband explains that, to a dog, once means always. Never means never.

The cartoon is the picture of consistency. Always or never. Never allow a dog to bite, especially if taking a treat from someone like a little child. Fingers can be damaged. Put a treat in your hand, make a fist, offer it to the pup, and say, "Don't bite." When the pup licks the hand for the treat, open your fist and offer the treat. I take it a step further by hiding a treat in extended fingers. I wouldn't do this with an adult dog that hasn't learned not to bite. A puppy generally doesn't bite too hard on this one, but it may try. You should say, "Lick," until the pup licks your fingers. Only after it successfully licks in lieu of biting should you offer up the treat.

Never let a big breed jump up on anyone. Small dogs often are lapdogs, but that is a different scenario. Letting a big dog jump as if it is a puppy can only lead to a possible tragedy when they grow up. A victim could be a feeble old person or an unsuspecting child. Injuries could result. To help your pup learn, bring your knee up when the pup jumps. It causes them to tumble backward. You also can walk into a pup and cause it to lose balance. Another method is just to turn away, although I have found my pups still will jump on my backside. Find whichever method works best to break this habit early. Be consistent.

Don't allow begging while the family eats at the table. Tell the pup "Don't beg … go to your rug!" and soon you will only need to say, "Don't beg." Of course, you have to be consistent with not letting anyone feed the pup from the table. Very young children are a little harder to help with that training. Tim and Mandy used to regularly offer food they didn't like to Boo. She made it her place to sit under their highchair at mealtime. We let that one slide. It made for a lot less clean-up time, but we were consistent.

When it comes to bad behavior, however, don't ever allow it. That's *never*. It can make the difference between life and death for your pup or adult dog. You never want a pup to be so lax with commands that they don't immediately recognize and obey a stern or yelled "No!" or "Stop!" or "Leave it!" It can prevent them from running into street traffic—or possibly stop them from eating a potentially toxic substance or medication that has fallen on the floor.

Staying out of the street has been fairly easy for my pups to learn. I walk them to the curb and point to the street and tell them, "No! Bad! Stay out of the street!" I make a point to spend extra time getting the mail from the curbside box, or weeding or hand trimming the vegetation next to the street. I give the pups plenty of opportunity to learn this life-saving command. As a city-dweller, I know this is important.

I remember the trauma as a young boy of watching one of our family dogs get hit by a car right in front of me. We had been playing in our front yard. The dog darted into the street and was struck as I watched. The dog died. I literally ran after the offending car, which didn't stop. I was going to make the driver pay for what he did. One of my older siblings chased me down nearly a block away. I never wanted to see that again. I never want another child to witness that horrific scene. Avoiding such heartbreak starts with the pup learning boundaries.

That is where tough love may come in. Extremely dangerous situations are the only times I might spank my pups during the learning process. By spank, I mean a swat on the bottom. It doesn't take much, and I don't use much force—just enough to make a statement. The rarity of the swat makes the statement all that much more pronounced. The boss means business. I wanted to spare their lives by making certain they understood some things are not allowed—ever. Consistency. The master needs to be just as consistent as the pup. It is essential for proper training.

Unfortunately, human masters are not perfect, and sometimes we make mistakes in our training. Furthermore, we might slip and let bad behavior go once in a while. We might be too shy to ask guests to help us by not allowing our puppies to jump on them, steal cookies from little children, beg at the table, or do anything else that should not be permitted.

Fortunately for us, our heavenly Master *is* perfect, and He is perfectly consistent. God doesn't change. He is always the same, always just, always there to help us learn how to do things right. Sometimes He lets us experience tough love, too. There are consequences to our improper actions—maybe not immediate ones, but there will be consequences. There is great assurance when we know we can count on something to always be the same. God is that something. His characteristics don't change. His Word doesn't change! His message doesn't change! His love for us doesn't change! God is good all the time!

If only I could be so consistent. People marvel at how good our dogs have been over the years. Our key has been having rules—and sticking by them. We try not to change. We ask our guests and neighbors to not allow bad behavior, and explain that we are trying to train a great dog—not an average one. Our family supports each other during the training, challenges each other to stay consistent, and tries to set our standards high. We are not satisfied with just good dogs. We want super dogs.

I also have to set my own standards high if I am to please my heavenly Master. I can sense the Holy Spirit in me telling me to avoid trouble. I can almost hear His voice telling me to "leave it" when I am tempted. I know it is for my own good to obey. God knows everything that is good and bad for me. I'm like a puppy. I don't always know, but I have learned to trust Him. I don't want to be just a good Christian in His eyes. I want to be a super Christian.

A good church family can help with that. A good Christian accountability partner can help you toe the line. If you know your weakness is eating too much popcorn at the movies, ask your accountability partner to ask whether you had the small or the large. It makes you think before you overindulge.

We all know our weaknesses when it comes to our walk in life. We have to be honest in our self-assessment—and then we need help in keeping our walk safe and out of trouble. We can't do it alone—no more than a pup could learn to stay out of the street without guidance and shepherding. Ask God to help. Ask Him to provide a good accountability partner. Don't be so self-assured that you think you are capable of fending off the temptations you will face. Many a good man and woman have fallen. Many a good dog has run into the street.

Certainly don't be fooled into thinking your poor decisions can't be fatal to your reputation, your relationships, and even your life. There are some serious threats out there we need to avoid. The Master is serious about this. There will be consequences.

Learn to be consistent in all you do—consistently good. Being good requires knowing the rules and having the discipline to follow them. It gets easier and is a lot less painful when you elect to do right every time. Think always or never.

Ornery pup dive-bombs Grandma Bella

Walking in Rebellion

I have always envied people who can walk with their dogs perfectly at heel, slack leash, or no leash. The dog is in perfect harmony with the master. It is as if they just want to be together. Some of them even seem to walk in step, completely in unison. Please forgive me, but I have coveted that.

Unfortunately, this is the one area where my dogs and I have had an issue. Have I mentioned that Labs are very trainable and intelligent, but are strong-willed by nature? I often half-jokingly recommend young couples to train a Labrador before they have children. It will teach them a lot about consistency, and a whole bunch about being challenged. It is most true for me when it comes to taking a walk with my Labs.

I love being outside with my dogs, but I have never found they want to walk *with* me. They'd rather bounce ahead of me, racing out to smell a tree for squirrels, check a bush for a rabbit or bird, or find a big stick to carry. Maybe they want to run ahead to make sure the way is safe. Somehow, I doubt that last one was a high priority for them.

Perhaps my patience is not sufficient to getting them to the stage of proper heeling. I guess the problem is as much my technique as anything else. It certainly has a lot to do with the infrequency of our walks. My first three Labs and I took only a few walks on leash. My arms and shoulders couldn't handle very many of those outings.

Labs are strong enough to pull down small trees, drag large cars (perhaps a slight exaggeration), and snap ropes or chains that might not have tensile strength exceeding five hundred pounds. A mortal man or woman stands little chance of holding back a really rebellious, grown Labrador that truly wants to go someplace.

One of our friends had a year-old Lab male that escaped from their yard. Their adult daughter chased down the eighty-five-pound dog and put a leash on the big boy in hopes of walking him home. He had other ideas, however, when he spotted another dog and wanted to go visit. He pulled the young woman off her feet and dragged her for several yards before the dog stopped. She was badly scraped and bleeding.

I was pulled off my feet more than once when I tried to teach Boo, as a young adult, to heel on leash. She was a hunter and wanted to blaze our trail. She was a great dog in the field and quickly learned she shouldn't get too far ahead of me while hunting. If she did and flushed a bird, I would have little chance of hitting it and she would have no chance of retrieving it. She learned it was better to give me the best chance possible of hitting something—the closer the better. I wasn't that talented a shot. She also would come back to me regularly just to encourage me to keep up. But put her on a leash? Not a good thing.

I never felt right about pulling on choke-chain collars or using one of the barbed pinch-collars intended to deter a dog from pulling too hard. My dogs would pull and gag and cough, sounding as if they were hanging from a noose. It never seemed quite right. With a regular collar—even as pups—they would simply squirm, pull, and eventually slip right out of the leather straps. It was easier to let them run and call them back occasionally to keep them out of trouble. I guess avoiding conflict is one of my character flaws—even with my dogs.

Leash laws, of course, made us quit taking walks in town. City walks weren't safe when the dog was running ahead. The new laws required dogs to be on a leash. Those long leashes provided no real control—and a short leash was a real workout for me when walking my girls. It was just too tiring and discouraging to keep trying. My shoulders hurt. I lost patience—and I always felt badly about that.

I wonder whether God gets that frustrated with us. He used to love to walk in the Garden with Adam, but then Adam and Eve started pulling on the leash. Instead of enjoying the walk and doing the proper thing, they rebelled. They ate from the forbidden tree. They ran into the street. As much as God, and even Adam, cherished those walks, the leash law was broken. Rebellion brought an end to those wonderful times of bonding.

I know there are times when I pull hard on the leash and slip out of the collar of righteous living God has fashioned for me. I would rather be off doing the things I think would be more fun—things that I shouldn't be doing, things from which the leash would protect me.

We think we have a better way and try to drag God along with us. God doesn't work that way. I have learned my leash is God's guidebook—the Bible. His instructions are meant to protect me, but I sometimes find myself fighting against the Master's lead because I think I know best.

One of the common thoughts from people who don't want any part of a Christian walk is that they don't want to abide by what they perceive to be strict lifestyle guidelines. They have to give up all the fun stuff in life. I was one of those when I was younger, too. Rules are made to be broken, right?

Lexi knows when she is crossing the line with me. She looks back at me because she figures some sort of correction is coming. For example, when my wife comes home from her long days as a real estate agent, Lexi waits at the top of the stairs, wagging and hopping. After Georgie puts down her purse and papers and sits on the couch, Lexi will begin to crawl up in her lap. Then she looks back at me. Lexi knows she will get her loving, petting, and hugging from Georgie, but crawling into her lap is just too big a temptation to pass up. However, all I have to do from across the room is clear my throat, and Lexi's paws slowly begin coming off the couch. She'll have to wait for lap time until my wife gets down on the floor with her, which generally follows a short time later.

In *God Is Closer than You Think*, John Ortberg writes about a similar human tendency. He refers to it as the "Don't look at me, God" times in our lives when we know we are doing—or are about to do—something wrong. We don't want God to look at us. We don't want Him to see us crossing the line. We don't want to feel the shame of being disobedient—at least while we are being disobedient.

King David found there is no place to hide from God. There is no place He cannot see or go. In Psalm 139:7–10, David said, "Where can I go from Your Spirit? Or where can I flee from Your presence. If I ascend to heaven, You are there; If I make my bed in Sheol, behold, You are there. If I take the wings of the dawn, if I dwell in the remotest part of the sea, even there Your Hand will lead me; And Your Right Hand will lay hold of me."

Adam and Eve messed up in the Garden and went into hiding. As Mandy said, "Like we can hide from God!" God knows when we mess up. He sees it. He is there.

I am not perfect. I'm just like Lexi in that I know who my heavenly Master is, and as I've grown in my walk with Him, I've learned His rules. I find myself looking over my shoulder at my Master when I know I am tempted to cross the line of disobedience. I have learned I might as well get my feet back where they are supposed to be because I'm really not going to enjoy what I thought I might.

I will be hearing, or at least imagining that I hear, God clearing His throat. I can envision Him raising an eyebrow and pointing a finger of warning as I do with Lexi. Do I really want to go there? When I stop and think—about the consequences, about who else might be watching, about destroying a witness to someone in need or breaking a trust that could crush a soft spirit, when I *really* think about it—it isn't so hard to pull my paws off the couch. That brief moment of fleeting enjoyment isn't worth it.

That is the very reason why some folks say they don't want to think about becoming a Christian. They can't have fun anymore. The rules are too abundant and too strict. I was one of those people a long time ago. I wanted to do the immature puppy thing—run after the rabbits, climb trees for squirrels, chew up the garden hose, and dig up the flowerbeds in the backyard.

As I grew older and matured in my thinking, I found that God's rules really are not meant to be restrictive. They are meant to be protective. When I live within those rules, when I stay in the yard and out of the street, I am generally pretty safe. When I challenge the rules, I often find trouble.

Our adult Sunday school classes have always had regular social potluck gatherings. Hey, we're Baptists, and Baptists do potluck. We eat.

At one of these socials many years ago, my wife invited a recently divorced friend of hers. The woman had felt alone and abandoned by her friends after the divorce. She didn't want to go the bar route to find new companionship, so she accepted my wife's invitation to a party—even of churchgoing people.

After the party, which included a few tame, but fun, adult games, the woman got in the car to ride home with us. She was smiling. "I never knew people could have that much fun and not drink a lick," she said. Yes, we Christians can be a fun bunch.

I have found delight in not tugging on the leash. It is so much more enjoyable when I walk with the Master without pressure.

The Apostle Paul once said he pulled against his leash, too. He found himself doing things he really didn't want to do and not doing the things he knew he should. (Romans 7:15)

It is our nature to walk in rebellion, to tug on the leash. I wonder if God's arms get tired at our tugging. I pray He never lets go.

Lexi walking in respect with Tom

Walking in Respect

Rewards are good, right? Don't we all want to get a bonus or pat on the back when we do something well? It encourages us to work hard, perform our duties with perfection, and strive to do things with excellence. When we hold proper respect for someone, we want to perform in order to receive a reassuring word or confirming pat. It works in our jobs and marriages—really in every relationship. As our respect for another person grows, we get to a point where we don't need the reassuring word or confirming pat. Our motivation changes and we just don't want to let that person down. Our own expectation for how we act and react is elevated—all on our own. We are all about pleasing. It is the maturing transformation from self to selfless—phileo love to agape love.

One thing I have learned over the years is that if you want respect, you have to earn it. I don't understand all the dynamics in how it works except that when you see a good person continuing to do well, it commands respect. In my mind, scoring points for respect is when I see someone respecting others, working hard without prodding or demanding accolades, caring for those in need, acting unselfishly, protecting the underdog, or maybe just generating a smile in times of crisis. It is easy to appreciate such a person.

Respect in the dog world means establishing yourself as pack leader, the one who sets the rules, and the one who demands consistent obedience. Once you have won that respect, much of your challenge in training is resolved. It becomes a matter of teaching the pup your language and what is expected of each command.

While consistency is of utmost importance, I still don't like to be too rigid in the very early training process. I don't think it is necessary to demand consistent obedience with a firm hand right off the bat with puppies. You want to earn their trust and respect—not break their spirit. Remember, they don't know the language or the rules. We first have to share the information in an understandable way. Rewards are a great incentive for a pup, particularly something tasty. It also works wonders for correcting bad behavior.

The young pup has to get over himself, which is kind of like the Apostle Peter, who had to eat some humble pie before he could set off to change the world for Christ. Peter was one of those "speak-without-thinking" kind of guys. He acted on impulse. He didn't always think before jumping in for all he was worth. He was a lot like most of us.

After he denied Jesus three times before Christ died on the cross, Peter was beside himself. He didn't realize he could fail so terribly by denying Jesus after all they had been through together. After Jesus rose from the grave, He visited with Peter again and asked the apostle three times if he loved Him. Peter basically answered, "Sure, I'm your good buddy" the first two times. They were using the "phileo" love of brotherhood. However, the third time Jesus asked the question, He changed the word "love" to "agape." Peter appeared to break. He changed his answer: "Jesus, You know I love (agape) you." Jesus did know Peter loved Him and now Peter was ready to do God's work with the right mindset. Peter then knew He loved Jesus, too. He moved from self to selfless.

I am convinced giving treats helps a pup get into the proper mindset for doing a trick and learning the language. It also can help me get past the rebellious walking with my dogs. I am certain if I stay committed and consistent for long enough, I'll have the dog walking obediently beside me—on leash or off. No tugging or pulling—just walking with me in respect and appreciation of being together.

Peter didn't get it right the first time, but Jesus stayed with him, helping him think through the process. Peter needed to know that

Christ was okay with him. Jesus offered the pat on the head, the reward, and the confirmation that turned Peter from a pebble in the faith to a solid rock. Peter gained a newfound, unquestioning respect for Jesus.

Lexi showed signs of changing her attitude about walking in respect to my wishes by the time she was six months old. I decided this aspect of her training should start earlier than it did with the other pups. With the first two Labs, I hunted often so they didn't learn to respect the leash at all. They would respect a voice command, but sometimes that I had to scream because they were hot on the bird trail about a half-mile ahead of me. I didn't hunt Sadie, but I didn't make an effort to walk much with her, either. My life was too busy with work and projects. That was my loss. She was a master-pleasing dog in that she liked to make me feel good by being obedient. I think she would have been an easy walker.

A nice lady who goes to our church is a professional dog trainer. She helps prepare service dogs by working with puppies. She gets the pups accustomed to behaving in crowds, walking through stores, and sitting quietly or lying down in church without whimpering or fidgeting. These puppies are impressive. They all seem to be so well mannered. She does a great job with them.

I asked her how I could get heeling down with a loose leash. She suggested something I had read about. When a pup starts to pull on a leash during a walk, change directions and go the other way. I didn't want to admit to her that I had tried it, but got really dizzy.

I also read that another technique was to just stop. The pup would eventually associate pulling with stopping. They really didn't want to stop so the premise was they would stop pulling. I bruised my heel and strained a hamstring while attempting the "stop-and-go" method. I am challenged when it comes to getting this "heel" thing down.

Lexi came along at a time in my life when I had time to take a couple of good, long walks each week during warm weather. I learned to carry a pocket full of small treats, which I offered her with some regularity as we walked along. While she might tug on the leash at the start of our walks, she would soon settle down and understand that there were rewards for walking where the master desired. Within a couple of minutes, she was walking beside me with no pressure on the leash. What fun! I was really enjoying this.

We would walk and talk. I'd pat her on the head every so often, telling her what a special puppy she was, and give her a treat to reward her for her obedience. Yes, I was buying her respect, but then one day I forgot the treats. Lexi acted a little disappointed at the beginning of our walk. She kept tapping her nose on the pocket where the goodies were supposed to be. All I had was a kind word and a pat on the head. After a short time, she began to understand. "Hey, this was pretty good anyway."

We had a breakthrough that day. The walk was most enjoyable—and there was respect on the end of the leash. There was no tugging. She was happy just to be with me—and I was delighted to be out there with her.

The Old Testament patriarch Jacob had the same kind of breakthrough walk on his way to find a wife from the family of his uncle, Laban. One night during his journey, Jacob had a dream. He saw a stairway to heaven, and angels were going up and down from heaven to earth. God was standing beside Jacob and told him He would go with Jacob and protect him. What reassurance Jacob must have felt knowing God would be walking with him.

It was a life-changing event for this man who had cheated his twin brother and lied to his father. Jacob still wasn't perfect, but his life changed out of respect for God. He was a better man for that walk. The pressure of life didn't seem quite so hard to handle after that night.

Before his fall, Adam had enjoyed his walks with the Master in the Garden. He had the Master's ear. Adam was getting a pat on the head, a kind word from God. He felt comfortable on those walks. He was respectful. "This was pretty good."

There are times in our spiritual walk when we feel really close to God. We are walking with a really good friend, someone we love, someone we respect, and someone who loves us much more than we realize. He is listening to our words. He is comforting and pleased when we aren't pulling on the leash. "This is really good."

Puppy love

Walking in Love

We all have our carrots in life—the incentives that help us do something. Dogs aren't any different. At first, it is usually a treat to help a new pup learn a trick. Do the trick and get a reward. It is one of the easy ways to teach a dog how to sit. Put a treat in your palm, let the pup smell it, close your hand, and move the closed fist over the pup's head. The pup follows the treat and automatically sits down. They sit, you tell them "nice sit," and they get a treat.

Sadie was really treat-oriented. The kids used to have fun teaching her something new—and she was eager to learn. It meant getting a puppy biscuit. One of us had taught Sadie to shake hands one afternoon, and we were excited to share that with other family members. Tim came home, and we told him Sadie had learned a new trick. He was anxious to see for himself so he grabbed a biscuit and sat down on the couch.

Before Tim said a word, Sadie bounced up and sat, lay down, sat back up, barked, reached out a paw to shake, lay down, sat, barked, reached out for a shake, and ran through the five tricks she knew for nearly three minutes as we all laughed ourselves silly. Tim still had not said a word. He was laughing too hard.

While treats are great incentives to get pups motivated to do their tricks, they eventually learned obedience didn't always get a treat. Sometimes it was just a pat on the head or some kind words. I think they soon learned to obey just because they loved us and wanted to please us. It went beyond the respect for the one holding the leash or expecting obedience for a command. It is a step beyond when you so respect someone that you don't want to let them down because you love them.

Boo was a great pleaser. She would learn new tricks quickly. Eventually she would do something for you because she wanted to please—not because she had to have a treat for a reward. She discovered early on that the more obedient she was, the more she was allowed to go with you or be with you—wherever that might be.

My dad was not one to believe a dog should be a house pet. We kids, of course, always begged to have a dog in the house. One summer on a family vacation to a resort in Minnesota, the camp owner held an evening barbecue for all those in his cabins. He had a cute longhaired Dachshund that seemed to shadow her owner. The little dog never seemed to get in trouble. She was good around kids and adults. She never barked at anyone. We soon found out how talented the little dog was, too.

As the man grilled hot dogs and burgers that evening, he grabbed one of the first hot dogs off the grill and handed it to his little dog. He said, "Here, take this, but don't eat it." The little dog took the warm, meaty delight and found a spot under a chair near the grill. She dropped the hot dog in front of her and drooled all over it for the next fifteen minutes until her master remembered and told her it was okay to eat it. She gobbled it down. That trick so impressed my dad that he said any dog trained well enough to do that would be good enough to be welcomed in his house.

I remembered dad's comment more than fifteen years later when Boo came along. We were about to travel back home for a visit and planned to take Boo along with us. She was used to sleeping with us inside every night so I anticipated how she might react if she weren't even allowed in my dad's house. We planned to be there for a few days. I figured I had to work on the hot dog trick. I wanted Boo to be welcomed by my dad.

Boo had learned to "hold it" with a training dummy as we learned hunting commands. She would hold the canvas dummy until I asked her to give it to me. If she could do that so well, holding a hot dog trick shouldn't be too tough, right?

The first hot dog I waved in front of her nose somehow managed to slip down her throat. I wasn't quick enough. I don't think she even chewed it. With the second hot dog, I told her before I gave it to her that she should *hold* this one. She acted as if she got the message as I placed the hot dog in her open mouth. I gently tapped her lower jaw as she strained to obey. She had the good taste of the first one and now the boss was giving her more. She was in heaven. This meaty thing was really good. She didn't want to make a mistake a second time. She might not get more.

I didn't make her wait long before I said okay. She quickly gulped it down. We practiced with dog biscuits for a few more days before heading back to visit the folks. I reminded dad of what he had said at the fishing camp. He remembered. I pulled a hot dog from the cooler. Boo held it until I told her okay. Dad was impressed. Boo slept by our bed that night—in my dad's house.

As she grew more mature, I could sense Boo was happiest when she was following orders. "Please, let me do something for you." To me, she was a living example of the word image you get reading Matthew 18:10. The last part of that verse tells us of angels continually facing the throne of God. It is a word picture of them eagerly waiting for God's commands so they could leap into action. They were anxious to do His bidding. "Go help the little ones around the world." "All right! Something special to do for the Master! We get to go help His children. Let's go."

I thought of how a good Lab sits facing his or her master, anxious for a command to go do something—fetch the ball, retrieve the newspaper, find your keys, do tricks, or come over for a hug. A really good dog is that anxious to please. Don't get me wrong—biscuits or a piece of bread still matter, but they are no longer the primary motivation. Pleasing out of love and respect now matters most.

Lexi proudly holds a treat

I also can imagine God looking down with a smile when His mission is accomplished by His angels—or by us. He is in a position to expect and demand obedience. Angels in His presence are so in love with their Master that there is nothing they wouldn't do for Him. They are eager to obey. They can't wait to fulfill His every wish. They don't need a biscuit. They just want to please. "Please, let me do something for You."

As I have matured and grown in my walk with God, I have learned so much about His love for me that I can't help but love Him back. "We love Him because He first loved us." (1 John 4:19) When we learn the extent of that love, being respectful and obedient is no longer a chore. It is a delight.

Unchallenged, unconditional, unchanging love is what God is all about. It is what Jesus showed us in His walk to the cross. He went obediently, knowing it was the Father's will. He also knew His mission had greater purpose than self. It was payment for our sins. That mission was greater than the pain and sacrifice He had to go through to get there. He did it in loving obedience for the Master. He did it so we could someday be in the presence of the Master. Sin separates us from God. Forgiveness through Christ restores us to a relationship with God. Great love saves us. Jesus suffered the cross because of His love for all of us.

Tom and Boo on her last hunt

When the Walk is Over

Every walk comes to an end. Sometimes when we have experienced a really good walk, we don't want it to end. We'd love to keep going. We feel great. The weather is wonderful. The day is not too cool and not too hot. Perhaps your walking partner is such a delight that you lose track of time and distance. Why not just keep walking?

It is almost a disappointment to have to stop on those days. Of course, we can't always keep going. Every good walk must come to an end. Life gets in the way of even the very best walk.

One of the very unpleasant lessons I have learned in life is that where there is great love, there can be great loss. That is especially true for our relationships. The greater the love, the greater the pain when we lose a special relationship through separation or death.

Boo was the first really great dog I raised, trained, and enjoyed. She was awesome in so many ways, such as stopping what she was doing when I so much as cleared my throat. She wanted to make sure she wasn't doing something she wasn't supposed to—or maybe was missing an opportunity to do something for me. Sometimes I just needed to clear my throat. She still stopped. She loved me enough to want what I wanted. I loved her a lot in return.

Our kids loved her, too. They had never known life without their dog. When she developed cancer, it was all we could do to scrape together funds to try to treat her. The veterinarian finally told us there was nothing more we could do but try to help her be comfortable in her final days.

She became so weakened by her disease that she would just stay on a rug at the top of the stairs near the door. When someone came home, her tail would signal her joy by thumping on the floor. Sometimes she couldn't even lift her head. We'd all get down and hug her as much as we could. When even that became painful for her, we had to let her go.

My own father had died at a young age a few years earlier. He had not yet had his sixtieth birthday when a series of heart attacks took him away from us. At the time of his death, I thought there could be no greater pain of loss than for this really good man who I loved and respected a lot. I took a walk by myself up on the hill of our old acreage a day after his funeral and had a really good talk with God about Dad. My dad had said the prayer of salvation years before, so I knew he was in God's presence as the Bible promised. I had never been one to cry, but the tears soon were flowing. Then God's peace came upon me. Dad was in good hands. I had an image of Sparky running up to him sideways with a great big smile. I had to smile, too, at the thought.

After leaving Boo at the vet's office on that last day we saw her, I recalled my talk with God about my dad. This was great loss, too. We couldn't have asked for a better dog. She was family. The tears again were flowing as I drove home to tell the kids, who had been at school. We all had a good cry and a prayer that God would take good care of her, that maybe she could find Grandpa and Sparky, and wait until we joined them.

Not yet a teenager, Mandy asked if dogs went to heaven. I believe they do. They are one of God's creations, and He tells us in His written word that all creation will be made new one day. If my theology is flawed on that one, I'd just as soon not know. I'd like to think good dogs get maybe a little extra consideration for the example of unconditional love they show us here. I sincerely doubt that one in truth, but, hey, someday we will find out for certain. I would love to see Boo again, and Pepper and Sadie, and Lexi, too, if I outlive her.

After Boo died, my wife said she could never have another dog because the pain of the loss was too great. She had great loss from great love. Why would you put yourself through that again? The answer is simple. We had eleven years of great love with a special dog. My wife saw the light. We then had nine years of great love with another dog, and then twelve years with another. We are enjoying several years already with our fourth.

Lexi is still a relative baby as of this writing. Our prayers are for her to live a long time with us and leave us with wonderful memories of another special bonding. She will leave us someday, too, and we will experience great loss again. Great loss only comes from great love.

God showed us that when He sent His Son to walk with us. Mankind had thirty-three years to enjoy a walk with the Son of God. They had an estimated three years of His ministry to tell us about the joy of walking with God, and the eternal joy to come. But when Jesus's time came, there was great loss from great love for Him as well.

As the Gospel messages intimate to us, He suffered the greatest loss of all. He not only sacrificed His life on the cross, He never knew sin yet accepted all our sins on that cross with Him. He cried in great pain when all that sin temporarily separated Him from the Father with whom He had always walked. God turned the earth dark at mid-day. It caused Him pain, too, if only for a moment of His eternal timeframe. For that brief instant, there was great loss because of the greatest love of all—a sacrifice on the cross so we who believe in Him might share in eternal life. That is a life forever walking with God, the giver of unconditional love.

Yes, I believe there are a great many parallels in our walk with our dogs and our walk with God. Starting life with a new puppy begins a love affair that can build a special relationship with so many potential rewards as we grow together over the years. It can be such a wonderful walk—one we can only hope will never end.

On an even grander scale is our spiritual walk in Christ, but that is an eternal journey of bountiful blessings that begins the day we accept Jesus as our Savior. And the best aspect of all—that walk never will come to an end.

God gives us all an invitation to take that walk, to experience His loving hand up close and personal. But to enjoy the walking, the loving, the touching, and the knowing, we first have to come.

When our puppies are young, it is one of the first commands they must learn. Generally we offer them a treat to encourage them to respond to our call. Soon we can just give the call, and they will respond. When they balk at the command, we might have to tie on a long leash and reel them in a few times while calling to them. It helps them grasp the discipline that when the master calls, we come. Once true obedience takes over, however, it becomes a command that is all but automatic.

God will call each and every one of us home to Him one day. It is a calling from which we will not be able to run. None of us will be able to avoid it or deny it. Some of us get to the point where we are eager to hear this call. Some might regret not listening to the calling earlier in this life.

My mother was in her eighties when she struggled with congestive heart failure. My dad had died nearly thirty years earlier, but she never remarried. She knew her true love, and that was good enough for her lifetime.

When a minister visited her in the hospital after one of her serious health flare-ups, he asked if she was afraid of dying. She answered quickly and confidently, "No." She knew where she was going and that was Heaven to be with her God and her husband. She had answered a call to come to Jesus earlier in her life. She knew about salvation and the promise of eternal life for those who believe in the Son of God. She had invited Him into her heart years before my dad confirmed to her that he had done so, too. She had no fear about where she was going. She would not be alone. She was ready to heed the call from God to come.

The losses we have in this life do indeed leave an empty place in our hearts. We miss the companionship, the love, the touch, the conversations, and the advice. However, we have something better to look forward to—life with the Master. He is waiting at the open door.

Dedication

To my wife, Georgie, and my children, Tim and Mandy, for their encouragement to write the book I have been pondering for some time. To my late parents, Howard and Betty, for my upbringing and impressing upon me the value of integrity, respect, and love for one another. To my dogs—Boo Boo, Pepper, Sadie, and Lexi—for just being my dogs and loving me.

Tom, Mandy and Lexi

About The Author

Tom Vint retired from The Associated Press in 2005 after a twenty-five-year career as a sports, broadcast, and news editor in Nebraska. He teaches adult Sunday school at Omaha's Westside Church. Tom authored *University of Nebraska: Finished Business—1994 National Champions,* for the Nebraska Cornhuskers' football season and coauthored the 1995 championship season book as well, both published by UMI Publications. Tom was outdoor-sports editor at the *Lincoln Journal and Star* from 1972 until 1980. It was there he first fell in love with his Labradors. Tom currently is a mortgage loan originator in Omaha. He has been married to Georgie since 1969. They have two children, Tim and Mandy.

Sources

"Pickles" cartoon by Ben Crane.

"Non Sequitur" cartoon by Wiley Miller.

God Is Closer than You Think, John Ortberg, Zondervan, 2005.

Hey Pup, Fetch It Up! Bill Tarrant, Sun Trails Publishing, Inc., 1979.